THE HOT SPRINGS COVE STORY

MICHAEL KAEHN

THE
HOT SPRINGS
COVE STORY

THE BEGINNINGS OF
MAQUINNA MARINE
PROVINCIAL PARK

HARBOUR
PUBLISHING

Harbour Publishing Co. Ltd.
P.O. Box 219, Madeira Park, BC, V0N 2H0
www.harbourpublishing.com

Edited by Cheryl Cohen   Indexed by Rebecca Pruitt MacKenney
Map by Roger Handling   Cover design by Anna Comfort O'Keeffe
Text design by Carleton Wilson
Cover photos: Raymond and Hugh Clarke at Hot Springs Cove, Michael Kaehn Family Collection;
    trail to the hot springs photo by Joyce Verma; Hot Springs Cove waterfall, from a postcard sent by
    Raymond Clarke to his sister Beverley, Michael Kaehn Family Collection.
Unless otherwise noted, all photos are from the Michael Kaehn Family Collection.

Printed and bound in Canada   Text printed on 30% recycled paper

Harbour Publishing acknowledges the support of the Canada Council for the Arts, which last year invested $153 million to bring the arts to Canadians throughout the country.

Nous remercions le Conseil des arts du Canada de son soutien. L'an dernier, le Conseil a investi 153 millions de dollars pour mettre de l'art dans la vie des Canadiennes et des Canadiens de tout le pays.

We also gratefully acknowledge financial support from the Government of Canada and from the Province of British Columbia through the BC Arts Council and the Book Publishing Tax Credit.

LIBRARY AND ARCHIVES CANADA CATALOGUING IN PUBLICATION

Title: The Hot Springs Cove story : the beginnings of Maquinna Marine Provincial Park / by Michael Kaehn.
Names: Kaehn, Michael, 1955- author.
Description: Includes bibliographical references and index.
Identifiers: Canadiana (print) 20190054875 | Canadiana (ebook) 20190054980 | ISBN 9781550178609 (softcover) | ISBN 9781550178616 (HTML)
Subjects: LCSH: Clarke, Ivan Harrison. | LCSH: Marine parks and reserves—British Columbia—Vancouver Island—History—20th century. | LCSH: Hot springs—British Columbia—Vancouver Island—History—20th century. | LCSH: Tourism—British Columbia—Vancouver Island—History—20th century.
Classification: LCC FC3815.M37 K34 2019 | DDC 333.78/3097112—dc23

Dedicated to my mother, Beverley Ivanetta (Clarke) Kaehn (1928–2008), who encouraged me to research her father's side of the family and over the years passed down to me every piece of her family history that she could remember.

CONTENTS

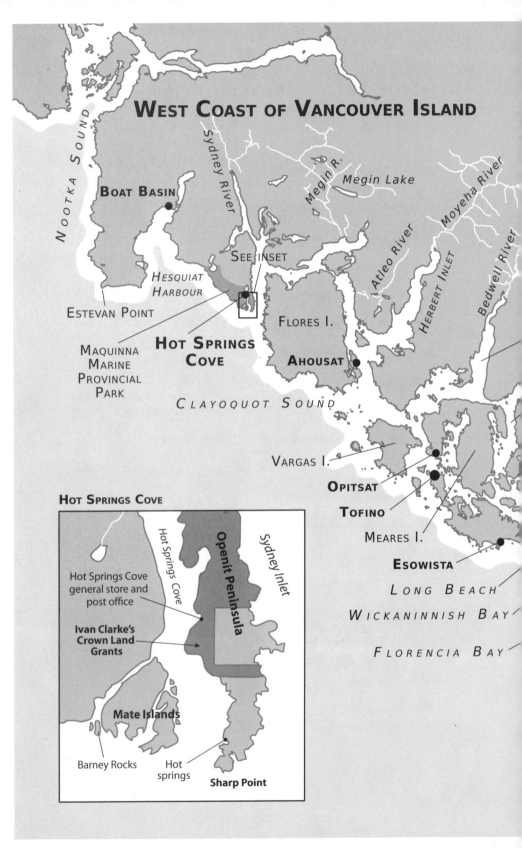

WEST COAST OF VANCOUVER ISLAND

NOOTKA SOUND

Sydney River

Megin R.

Megin Lake

Moyeha River

BOAT BASIN

Atleo River

HERBERT INLET

Bedwell River

SEE INSET

HESQUIAT HARBOUR

ESTEVAN POINT

FLORES I.

HOT SPRINGS COVE

MAQUINNA MARINE PROVINCIAL PARK

AHOUSAT

C L A Y O Q U O T   S O U N D

VARGAS I.

OPITSAT

TOFINO

MEARES I.

ESOWISTA

L O N G   B E A C H

W I C K A N I N N I S H   B A Y

F L O R E N C I A   B A Y

HOT SPRINGS COVE

Hot Springs Cove

Sydney Inlet

Openit Peninsula

Hot Springs Cove general store and post office

Ivan Clarke's Crown Land Grants

Mate Islands

Barney Rocks

Hot springs

Sharp Point

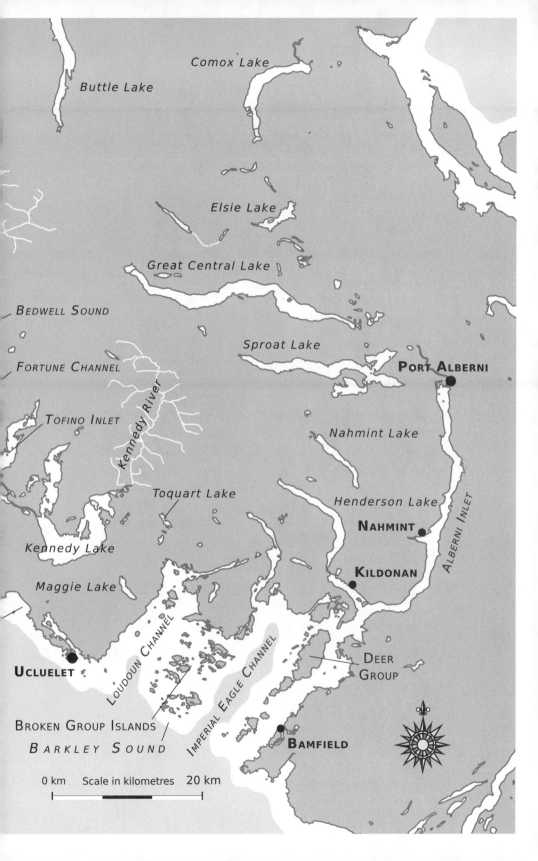

Ivan H. Clarke at Hot Springs Cove, drawn by Mort Graham for the Victoria Daily Colonist.

PREFACE

Iconic Ivan Harrison Clarke, born and raised in Victoria, had an exceptional, ambitious, enterprising personality. He held many positions in his life including corner store employee, farm worker, seaman, deckhand, mate, tugboat captain, seashell-crushing business owner, fruit and vegetable wholesaler, proprietor of a magazine shop, supply/store boat operator, general store owner, restaurant owner, Standard Oil agent, owner of a fish-buying camp, fur buyer, airline agent, unofficial banker, BC Telephone Company agent and member of the chamber of commerce of Tofino, as well as leading citizen and general factotum-in-chief. He also held several government-type positions— chief observer of aircraft, naval reporting officer, deputy receiver of shipwrecks, harbour master, wharfinger, Dominion government telegraph agent, postmaster, school trustee, deputy registrar of voters and unofficial mayor. When I was growing up I knew him as "Grandpa up the coast."

During my years of research for this book I came across certain words with alternative spellings that have been freely interchanged over the years. One of these is Sydney/Sidney. Sydney Inlet is about halfway up the west coast of Vancouver Island, and Sidney is on the northern end of the Saanich Peninsula on southern Vancouver Island. I have corrected Sidney to Sydney, except in quoted material. Ahousaht/Ahousat (pronounced A-hows-at) and Hesquiaht/Hesquiat (Hes-kweet or Hes-kwee-it) are often used incorrectly. The "aht" refers to the people, and the "at" ending denotes their village site.

Enjoy!

—M.A.K.

First Nations, Sailors, Investors: Discovering the Hot Springs

Before the world of tourism would come to know anything about the unique hot springs on the rugged west coast of Vancouver Island, they were known to the people of the Nuu-chah-nulth First Nations who had been living in the area since time immemorial. *Mok-she-kla-chuk*, or "smoking water," is the traditional Nuu-chah-nulth name for the hot springs, which were long used for sacred healing and other purposes. The name well describes why the springs have always held a certain fascination. Even these days, in the right weather conditions, steam can be seen hanging over the rocks in lazy smoke-like drifts where hot water bubbles up on the southeast corner of Hot Springs Cove in British Columbia, northwest of Tofino.

The rocks comprising the hot springs are said to date back more than 160 million years. The water is hot because surface water flows through a geological fault where the water is geothermally heated and pushed back to the surface by hydrostatic pressure, erupting at the surface through a fissure only 6 inches (15 cm) wide. The hot springs flow out of the fissure into a short stream that tumbles over a roughly 10-foot (3-m) waterfall into the first of six successive pools. The rising steam is sometimes visible to passing boats, especially on cooler days.

People from the Nuu-chah-nulth First Nations traditionally made their way to the Refuge Cove area (now Hot Springs Cove) to fish and gather resources for the upcoming winter. They drank water at the spring and took some home for medicinal reasons and to cleanse their bodies. Years ago it was also not uncommon to see Nuu-chah-nulth women doing their family laundry in the stream. They would lay their clothes out on shrubs and bushes to dry while the families showered under the waterfall. The Nuu-chah-nulth continue to live on their traditional land to this day. By the late 1700s—and continuing well into the 1800s—the location of the hot springs was gradually becoming known, and sailors, soldiers and other personnel of sailing ships from foreign countries had found and were making good use of them. The ships were small and the quarters crowded. After a long sea voyage, the visitors would get into longboats and row ashore at Refuge Cove then hike along what would have been a primitive trail to the springs. A steaming bath with unlimited hot water to wash their clothes in was exactly what they needed; in fact to them it must have felt like a godsend.

The number of visible pools may have changed over time. Ocean levels on Vancouver Island's west coast were about 10 feet (3 m) below their present level about seven or eight thousand years ago, and about 10 feet higher than their present level five thousand years ago, according to Jacob Earnshaw of the University of Victoria's department of anthropology. Lower ocean levels might have exposed more natural pools for the spring water to flow through and higher levels would have submerged the lowest two or three pools that are visible today.

Either scenario could also have made water access to the hot springs easier in earlier times than is the case today, where visitors follow a 1.25-mile (2-km) boardwalk from the cove to get there, whether they arrive by float plane or boat.

The fact that there were hot springs at all meant that entrepreneurs began showing an interest first in the water and then the land from around 1898, but for various reasons early plans fizzled. (See chapter 8.) Finally, though, in 1927, the Crown granted Robert Waugh Wyllie of Vancouver 20 acres (8 hectares), which included the land the hot springs were on, for $200. None of the families that settled in Hot Springs Cove remembers meeting Robert Wyllie over the years, but he did continue to retain ownership of the property.

What Wyllie did not own was the land containing the trail to the hot springs, which was needed because, for the most part, the rugged coastline close to the hot springs did not provide a good place for beaching boats. And that is where the adventurous Ivan Clarke of Victoria—my grandfather—entered the picture and set in motion the chain of events that would much later lead to the creation of Maquinna Marine Provincial Park.

For one of his numerous business ventures, Ivan leased a store/supply boat from his commercial fisherman friend, Adolphus Prince, in 1931. The boat had been converted from Prince's almost new 1930 fish-packer called the *Violet P*. Ivan sold groceries (including canned items, produce and dry goods), confectionaries and supplies up and down the west coast of Vancouver Island from Victoria to at least as far north as Zeballos, and quite possibly as far as Port Alice in the summer season, stopping at small communities, camps in small inlets and isolated cabins that the larger steamers did not service.

It was while stormbound on the *Violet P*. with some forty or so fishermen in Refuge Cove that he was first struck by the opportunity to start a new business in that remote and lonely cove. With the additional prospect of trade with the Nuu-chah-nulth people, coupled with the added attraction of the hot springs, Ivan thought it would be a good place for a land-based trading post/general store.

Refuge Cove was a convenient stopping place for mariners and the hot springs made it that much more attractive. Other than the occasional supply boat that dropped by, such as Ivan's, there was no one permanently situated in the area selling food and merchandise to those safely anchored in the cove waiting out the Pacific storms. The cove was one of the safest and handiest anchorages from bad weather on the entire west coast of Vancouver Island, and in 1933 Ivan decided to make his dream a reality. He went to the Land Registry office in Victoria, making Crown Grant applications on Clayoquot Land District Lots 1371 and 1372, the latter of which included the primitive trail to the hot springs.

The provincial government's Vancouver Island Settlers' Rights Act of 1904 allowed people to acquire provincial Crown land by claiming it for "settlement and agricultural purposes." Although it wasn't a requirement to live on the land itself, it was expected that all pre-empted land would be cultivated. In reality, the pre-emption system would never work on this part of Vancouver Island's west coast, as due to the soil conditions, there was little chance of being able to cultivate enough land to pass the pre-emption requirements, which earlier settlers in the area had already informed the government of as far back as the 1890s. For the time being, though, it gave Ivan the right to settle on the land and build a log cabin and store, and gave him full title to any timber, precious metals and coal on and under his land.

That autumn, Ivan, now thirty years old, with his pre-emption papers in hand, had secured mail-order accounts with the necessary wholesalers in Victoria. He purchased about $500 of grocery stock and merchandise that he knew he would be able to sell in his new general store. Along with $200 in his wallet, and his two dogs, an Airedale and a collie, he arrived on the BC Coast Service SS *Princess Maquinna* at Matilda Inlet, near Ahousat on Flores Island, southwest of Refuge Cove. (The ship was named after the famous Mowachaht chief Maquinna, born on Vancouver Island around 1760. The Mowachaht First Nation is part of the Nuu-chah-nulth First Nations.)

From there, Ivan was able to hire some men from the Ahousaht First Nation to take him, his dogs and supplies out to his new home in their boat. Refuge Cove was part of Canada's only true northern temperate coastal rainforest, containing virgin old-growth trees when Ivan arrived. After cutting down some alder trees that were in the way not far above the high-tide mark, he pitched his large canvas tent about midway up along the east shore of Refuge Cove on Openit Peninsula and settled in for the night. The peninsula is over 2 miles (3.2 km) long and varies from 1,000 to 4,000 feet (300–1,200 m) wide. It is composed of granite rocks with large, glacially smoothed outcroppings, with an average elevation of about 115 feet (34.5 m) above sea level.

That first night a cougar made off with his collie, leaving the Airedale and Ivan on their own. The next morning, Ivan nailed his general store sign to one of the trees in the small cluster at the end of his tent. All this activity drew many inquisitive members of the Nuu-chah-nulth First Nations and a number of fishermen, who purchased almost half of his supplies by noon that day.

The Iconic Ivan Clarke:
Early Years

Ivan Harrison Clarke was born on Monday, October 19, 1903, in Victoria, BC. He was the youngest child of William Harrison Clarke and Annie Emma (Carlow) Clarke, both of whom had coincidently arrived in Victoria on August 14, 1877, on the first-class steamship *City of Panama*, William a bachelor and Annie a spinster. The two were moving west from Ontario and New Brunswick respectively, via the first transcontinental train across America from Council Bluffs, Missouri, and then by ship from San Francisco. William with his cousin, and Annie with her extended family, were planning to start new lives.

Ivan was the twelfth child born to William and Annie, and the tenth to survive past infancy. In 1915, before Ivan's teenage years, his elder sister Cora Maude killed her husband, George Anderson, with the blunt side of an axe in the middle of the night, and then drowned herself the next morning by walking out into the nearby ocean by the seawall at Holland Point off Dallas Road in Victoria. This murder-suicide was local front-page news at the time, but the true story behind this now 100-year-old event has never been revealed publicly. Because it was one of those skeletons in the closet that until recently was still being kept quiet by close family members, it made this side of the family difficult to research.

William Harrison Clarke and Annie Emma Carlow met while travelling west to Victoria, William with his cousin and Annie with her extended family. They were married three months later.

While many of his older siblings were named after relatives and had rather English-sounding names, somehow Ivan stood out from the rest. His name wasn't English-sounding at all and there were no Ivans going back two hundred years in either his mother's or his father's families.

There is much family speculation about how Ivan came to acquire his name. At the time of his arrival in the world, it was the father's duty to fill in the particulars on the birth registration form, otherwise a reason for not doing so had to be given on the form. The family story passed down from my great-grandmother Clarke says that William went off to register his new son's name with Edward M. Fort, chief clerk at the Land Registry office, where all births, deaths and marriages were registered at that time, but by the time he got to the registry office he had forgotten what the name was. He improvised and supposedly named his youngest son after a good friend at work, and for the middle name used his own, Harrison, which had been the birth surname of his paternal grandmother. A birth announcement for Ivan did not appear in either of the Victoria newspapers.

The spelling of the Clarke name was originally different. William Clarke's last name was spelled "Clark" at birth. But in 1886, when he and Annie moved back to Victoria after some years of living in other places, there were suddenly two William H. Clarks in the city. Having difficulties getting his mail, William decided to add an "e" to the end of his name. This ended up being only a short-term cure to his mail problems, because a few years later another William H. Clarke appeared in Victoria. He was the manager of the Singer Sewing Machine Company store.

When Ivan entered the world, he instantly became an uncle to four nieces and nephews. Even as a small child, he insisted they call him Uncle Ivan, much to their displeasure. By the time he was ten he had eighteen nieces and nephews to reign over, with more on the way. Additionally, he already had sixty-two first cousins when he was born. Over the years, that count rose to eighty-three, not including the five who passed away at a young age. No wonder, when I was growing up, my mother always wanted to know who my female friends were, just in case we were related—even though Ivan's own maternal great-grandparents were first cousins. (This was a not uncommon practice in rural New Brunswick in the early 1800s, when there were not enough unrelated potential brides and bridegrooms to choose from.) Ivan's great-grandparents' marriage means that I am my own sixth cousin, and also a cousin to my daughters, and all of my ancestors and their siblings. Since Ivan's great-grandparents got together, there have been several other documented marriages of first cousins in this branch of the Carlow family.

In March 1910, when he was six years of age, Ivan and his mother left for New Brunswick on the Canadian Pacific Railway to visit Carlow relatives for several months. They stopped in both directions to visit his father's Clark and Jackson relatives in Bruce Mines, southeast of Sault Ste. Marie, Ontario. On the eastbound leg of the journey, Ivan visited his Clark grandmother for the first time, but sadly she passed away before they started their return trip west. They arrived home just before Ivan's elder sister Laura and her family moved east to Stony Plain, Alberta.

In 1911, William's youngest sister, Ida Hamilton, her husband, Will, and their three-year-old daughter, Margaret, moved in with Ivan's family temporarily after arriving from Butte, Montana, to make their home on the West Coast.

Nine older siblings had already entered school by the time Ivan started Grade 1, so he had something of a hard act to follow. But at Spring Ridge School in June 1912, he was awarded the Division I top "Deportment" award, meaning he had very good personal conduct and behaviour. At Hillside School in June 1913, he received an award for "Regularity and Punctuality," for not being late or missing one day of school during the term, an award he received again in June 1914. When he was old enough, he started working

Ivan, far right, was the youngest of William and Annie Emma Clarke's twelve children. He is pictured here with his four older brothers and father, at far left, in front of their home in Victoria, circa 1911. Sheelagh (Clarke) Varga Family Collection

part-time in his brother George's grocery store, which was near the Clarke family home.

When Ivan was a boy, raising chickens was just a fact of life, but he did very well with his chickens: newspaper clippings show that in early January 1912, he won several top prizes with his Single Buff Leghorn chickens at the 27th Annual Victoria Poultry and Pet Stock Show in the BC Agricultural Grounds buildings, which was then located on the Willows Fairgrounds in Oak Bay. Later that same month, at the first annual Provincial Poultry Show in Vancouver, his hen won first place in competition with chickens of the same breed from all over the continent.

Alberta attracted another of Ivan's siblings in 1913, when his oldest sister, Annie, and her family moved to Carvel, west of Edmonton. They farmed in Alberta until 1926, then returned to the coast to live in Vancouver. In 1920, Ivan was working as a farmhand and living with his parents on his brother Albert's 25-acre (10-hectare) farm, "Lovelands," at the south end of Beaver Lake, in the Royal Oak district of Saanich, BC. Albert also owned two farms near Edmonton. Quite possibly, they were the farms his sisters lived on.

Off to Sea

Toward the end of 1920, after Ivan had turned seventeen, he started working on local tugboats with his brother-in-law, Captain James (Jim) Olson, whose mentoring gave Ivan the opportunity to obtain his tugboat captain's papers very early in life. Jim, originally from Sweden, was one of the best and most experienced tugboat masters around. He was a former sealer out of Victoria, and served on several vessels before pelagic sealing was abolished in 1911. Jim would have known the same Clayoquot Sound general store/trading post merchants and former Nuu-chah-nulth seal hunters who Ivan would one day hear of, or cross paths with.

Jim became a West Coast tugboat master (skipper) for George McGregor's Victoria Tug Company. While working for Victoria Tug, Jim successively served as master of the 68-foot tug ss *Sadie* built in 1892, the 81-foot 9-inch ss *Strath* built in 1926 and the ss *Swell*—all tugs that Ivan was to work on as well.

During the World War I years of 1914 to 1918, when most experienced sea-men signed up to go to war, the local towboat companies, like Victoria Tug, had brought in a new hiring policy. They started hiring high school students who, if they stayed at sea for three years, could then work at obtaining their mate and eventually their master certification. The pay—and the life—was good, and they were being trained for and on Canadian ships. On the tugs they learned more about the British Columbia coastal waters than they would on larger vessels. The policy of hiring high school students, who proved themselves to be good workers, overall benefited the local towboat companies.

Prohibition in BC (1917–21) was still in place when Ivan started working on the tugs, which greatly helped the towboat business. Before prohibition was introduced, deckhands and firemen would last about a month, drinking up their earnings. During Prohibition, they worked many months and were able to send money home to their wives and children or their parents.

When Ivan started working on the tugs, diesel began to replace the original coal-fired steam engines. After the conversion, the tugs no longer needed the fireman position on board, and it became more economical to run a tug. The new engines took up less space on board than the steam plant, and they hardly needed any attention while the engine was running. With their new diesel engines, the tugs were much more competitive than the steam-powered tugs.

A diesel-powered tug was also no longer required to abide by the long list of government steamboat regulations and exhaustive inspections, which resulted in the owners of the tugboats having to pay for expensive refits whether they could afford them or not. A new diesel, costing many thousands of dollars, would make the tugboat owner think twice before investing that much money in an old hull, unless it was going to last for many more years of service.

The bad news was that the original steam engines were also used for powering the winches for the towing cables, as well as the anchors, and it did not make sense to have to install a new boiler just to operate the winches. To solve this problem, a long metal shaft was installed just below the deck and ran almost the entire length of the tug; those operations could then be performed using a series of chain gears and a clutch. Another downfall was that locally the tugs hauled a lot of coal for large coal companies, so there was an expectation that the tugs would use coal as fuel.

In his first couple of years tugboating, Ivan held various positions on several boats. In early 1921, he was a seaman, which was considered an entry-level position, with his brother-in-law, Jim, on George McGregor's 70-foot tug ss *Swell*, built in 1912 for McGregor's Victoria Tug Company. McGregor had the largest towboat business in Victoria at that time. Ivan also worked with Jim on McGregor's ss *Sadie* and ss *Strath*, plus the ss *Lorne*, owned by Hecate Strait Towing Company. The 151-foot *Lorne* was built for the Robert Dunsmuir collieries business on Vancouver Island in 1889. When it was built it was the biggest, strongest and most expensive tugboat in the area.

In 1922, Ivan and his parents had moved from the Lovelands farm back into town to Blanshard Street between Bay Street and Hillside Avenue. By the end of that year, Ivan had moved up from seaman to deckhand, which had more responsibility while the boat was underway. He handled lines and assisted with all operations on deck, including docking/undocking and the making and breaking of the various tows. He then became mate, second in command to the master. As mate he was responsible for deck operations and maintaining a safe navigation watch. He also assisted the deckhand in handling all lines, cables and the towing equipment for the tug as well as its tow. At various times he worked on the same tug as his nephew, Floyd Olson, who was one year younger than Ivan. For most of 1924, Ivan was a mate on William Gardner's Redstack tug, the 58-foot ss *Edna Grace*, built in 1903. The boat was renamed the *Island Comet* in 1928 after it was bought by Ivan's future brother-in-law, Harold Elworthy, owner of Island Tug & Barge Company Ltd.

Workforce shortages during World War 1 allowed high school students like Ivan, shown swabbing the deck, to learn the tugboat business.

Youngest Steamboat Master

In early November 1924, after being trained and mentored by his brother-in-law, Ivan was tested and he wrote and received his Certificate of Competency as Master of Steam Tug Boats. Having just turned twenty-one years of age, he was the youngest person to become a master mariner on the West Coast, and quite possibly in all of Canada and the United States. With the advent of diesel engines, that record may or may not still stand to this day.

The first tug he was master of was the 49-foot 5-inch SS *Respond* built in 1913, owned by Gardner Tug and Scow. It was rebuilt and converted to

Ivan's family was very proud of their master mariner. This painting of his first command was inscribed, "Ivan Clarke was twenty-one years old when he had his skipper's papers. Towboat Respond *built in Victoria, BC."* Foster Family Collection

The January 28, 1925, ship's manifest for the Respond *at Port Angeles lists Ivan as a master with three and a half years of experience at sea, the least of all the crew members.* National Archives and Records Administration, Washington, DC

diesel in 1931 and was renamed the *Island Trooper* in 1944, long after it had also become part of the Island Tug & Barge fleet.

In 1925, Ivan was the master of Gardner's 61-foot 6-inch SS *Hopkins*, built in 1909 by Hopkins Brothers Limited at Hopkins Landing, BC. The *Hopkins* was the largest and most ostentatious craft that had been built up to that time in Howe Sound. The *Hopkins* became part of the Island Tug & Barge fleet in 1926 and was later renamed *Island Rover*. Later that same year Ivan became the master of the *Edna Grace*.

Later, Ivan became the master of the SS *Swell*, and then of the 67-foot 2-inch SS *Burrard Chief* built in 1919, at that time owned by Island Tug & Barge. As well, he was master on their 50-foot 9-inch SS *Quinitsa*, built in 1914.

Ivan, photographed enjoying his pipe outside the SS Hopkins wheelhouse, became the boat's master in 1925. The following year the Hopkins joined the Island Tug & Barge fleet, started by Ivan's future brother-in-law, Harold Elworthy.

When it was completed in 1909, the Hopkins, *shown here in a mural by Bill and Chris Hart, was the largest craft to be built in Howe Sound.*

Serious Business

Harold Elworthy, Ivan's future brother-in-law, had started as an office boy at Arthur C. Burdick's Pacific Coast Salvage Company in 1918 and worked his way up, which gave Harold first-hand knowledge of the working of a shipping enterprise, and the local waters. In May 1925, with $125 to his name, twenty-four-year-old Harold borrowed $12,000 from the bank and, along with Captain Charles Coulson and his brother Britton Coulson, entered into a partnership to form Victoria's newest barge and towing business. With some of that money they purchased the 50-foot 9-inch tug ss *Quinitsa* from Captain Hume Blackley Babbington out of Prince Rupert, changing the tug's name to *Island Planet* in 1929.

Along with the Coulsons' 44-foot 4-inch tug ss *Della C*, also built in 1914, and a brand new 34-foot by 96-foot, 500-ton capacity barge, at that time the largest in local waters, that was the start-up of their towboat firm, Island Tug & Barge Limited of Victoria. It would become a major part of Ivan's life. Ivan was one of the first tugboat masters to work for Island Tug & Barge and he worked there for the rest of his towboating career.

On Saturday, May 23, 1925, Island Tug & Barge set up office on the old Hudson's Bay Company wharf at the bottom of Fort Street. Forty-eight-year-old Charles Coulson, who was also from Victoria, had been operating tugboats out of Prince Rupert and the Queen Charlotte Islands (now Haida Gwaii) for the previous fifteen years, giving him a thorough knowledge of those waters as well as the island's west coast. His thirty-seven-year-old brother, Britton, had also been working on tugboats.

By most accounts, the *Quinitsa's* first job as the flagship for Island Tug & Barge was towing a boom of logs from Sooke to Victoria for $125. By November 1925, Island Tug owned four tugs, adding the ss *Burrard Chief* and the 45-foot tug ss *Nora*, built in 1889, to their fleet along with twelve barges.

Island Tug built the first Davis Raft of logs towed out of Nootka on the west coast of Vancouver Island in 1933. The Davis Raft is a type of log boom that could be up to 250 feet long, 60 feet wide, and 30 feet deep (75.8×18×9 m), a cigar-shaped bundle held together with tons of cable, containing up to two million feet of logs. Invented in 1909 and patented in 1915 by Otis G. Davis and his brother, Mathew J. Davis, the Davis Raft is a method of transporting logs across the exposed waters off the island's west coast instead of the traditional wide, flat log boom people are so familiar with, which is used to tow

Ivan assumed command of the ss Burrard Chief, *part of the Island Tug & Barge fleet, in 1927. He was one of the first tugboat masters to join the company and spent the rest of his tugboating career there.* B.J. Elworthy Collection

logs in protected waters, but unfortunately would break apart in the open water.

Island Tug quickly grew and over the years became one of the largest employers in Victoria and the largest towboat company on the western hemisphere, gaining a place in nautical history for making numerous incredible—now famous—long-distance and deep-sea tows and salvages, which were closely followed by the newspapers, radio stations and, later on, TV stations of the time. In the middle of May 1926, Island Tug & Barge bought up all of the assets of Gardner Tug and Scow and Ivan found himself working for Island Tug & Barge.

Painted smoke stacks on tugs were used for recognition purposes. All Island tugs were easily distinguishable from any distance by their red-painted smoke stack with a black band on top. In the mid-1930s, the Victoria first-place Intermediate "A" boys basketball team sponsored by the company was even called the Island Tug Redstacks. "Redstack" was previously the name used to describe William Gardner's tugs before they were absorbed into Island Tug. It was normal for Island Tug to wait until their newly acquired tugs came in for a major refit of some kind before they were renamed, which could sometimes take several years.

Harold made sure the costs of his tug and barge services were fair both to the big companies and the smaller outfits. This guaranteed their continued patronage. In Ivan's early years, many of the local tows could have originated in Victoria, Sooke, Port Renfrew, Chemainus, Ladysmith or Vancouver, and might have ended up in Port Angeles, Anacortes, Bellingham, Seattle or Tacoma. At that time a lot of coal was being shipped out of Ladysmith by barge, as well as log booms being towed up and down the coast to the different sawmills in British Columbia and south of the border. After the logs were milled, fully loaded wood chip scows were then towed away, along with fully loaded lumber barges and scows. There were also scows loaded with sand, gravel or general cargo being towed, as well as the towing and docking of vessels of all sizes. More distant tows at that time would have gone right up the east and west coast of Vancouver Island and the mainland.

Uncharted Waters:
Business and Marriage

It was in his early twenties, while gainfully employed as a tugboat master, that Ivan started to show off his entrepreneurial personality by coming up with his first business venture, which revolved around crushing seashells. Within sixteen months he would be entering another new phase in his life: marriage.

The *Daily Colonist* of Tuesday, May 11, 1926, included the following small item on the business side of things:

> In approving the application for a galvanized iron frame building just west of the Rock Bay Bridge for Mr. Ivan H. Clarke, it was stated to the City Council last evening that it would be used for a shell crushing industry, the material being taken there by scow.

The article ran under the heading "Unusual Industry," so right from the start it was apparent Ivan did not have any local competition in this venture. He had full access to the tugs and the scows required to move the seashells, so it was easy for him to bring in the necessary shells. Arranging for an emptied barge to come back to the harbour with a load of some sort would have been a bonus for his employer. The site where he wanted to erect his building was just up the waterway from where all the tugs were moored in Victoria's upper harbour.

Shells could very reasonably be obtained from businesses harvesting oysters and clams on the east or west coast of the island. These shells are predominantly composed of calcium carbonate, which has several uses. Ivan's crushing plant could sell the crushed oyster shells for use in animal feed, especially for poultry to help with the production of eggs, and also for livestock feed and soil enrichment.

Mulching with crushed shell provides plants with much-needed calcium and minerals as the shells decay. The clamshells could also be used as a base for driveways and garden paths. For this venture he probably had some long chats with his brother George, who owned a chicken farm in Metchosin and would have known the initial contacts that Ivan needed to sell his crushed shells. Ivan would have also chatted with his tugboat boss, Harold Elworthy. Whether or not the crushing business ever got off the ground, much less lasted, is uncertain, but a few years later Joseph Heaney Ltd. on Wharf Street in Victoria ran a newspaper ad selling "Pure White Crushed Sea Shell for your garden paths or garage entrance."

Ivan and Beatrice

On the romance front, the *Daily Colonist* of August 21, 1927, included a notice that "Mr. and Mrs. Albert McDonald announce the engagement of their daughter, Beatrice Florence, to Captain Ivan H. Clarke. The marriage will take place in the near future."

Five days later, the newspaper ran another notice under the heading "Miscellaneous Shower," which began:

A miscellaneous shower was held Monday evening at the home of Capt. And Mrs. J.F. Olson, 2586 Cook Street, in honour of Miss Beatrice McDonald, a popular bride-elect, whose marriage will take place shortly. The gifts were concealed in a large basket prettily decorated in pink and white. Pink roses were used for the table decorations, and a three-tier wedding cake occupied the centre of the table. The evening was spent in music and games. Mrs. Hamilton, Mrs. McDougall and

Mr. James Williams were the lucky winners in the guessing contest, after which refreshments were served.

The following month, on September 2, Ivan and Beatrice were married in the Clarke family's church in Victoria. The *Daily Colonist* society page reported:

A quiet wedding took place at the Centennial United Church on September 2, when Rev. J.P. Westman united in marriage Beatrice Florence, daughter of Mr. and Mrs. Albert McDonald, and Captain Ivan Harrison, youngest son of Mr. and Mrs. W.H. Clarke. The bride was

Ivan and Beatrice were married in Victoria on September 2, 1927. They likely met through Harold Elworthy, Beatrice's brother-in-law and Ivan's tugboat boss.

attended by her sister, Mrs. Harold Elworthy, while Mr. Elworthy supported the groom. Among the many handsome wedding presents received was a case of cutlery from the firm of Oppenheimer Brothers, with whom the bride was employed, and a silver tea service from the Island Tug & Barge Company, the employers of the groom. Captain and Mrs. Clarke left immediately after the ceremony on the Vancouver boat and will spend their honeymoon on the Mainland and on their return will make their home in Victoria. The bride travelled in a pretty dress of rosewood taffeta silk with hat en suite and silver muskrat fur coat with a fox collar.

It's likely that Ivan and Beatrice had met through Harold. Ivan's tugboat boss was now officially his brother-in-law.

Almost three months after the marriage, Ivan's parents, William and Annie Clarke, celebrated their fiftieth wedding anniversary surrounded by their nine children in their home on Blanshard Street, with Annie wearing the brooch and earrings that William had given her on their wedding day. Forty of their fifty years of married life had been spent living in Victoria. Their daughters Laura Lory and Elsie Kinnear travelled from Alberta for the event, and their daughter Annie Barker and their son Albert came over from Vancouver. At that time, William and Annie had twenty-two grandchildren and six great-grandchildren.

Heroic Action

In 1928, Ivan was working as a master for Island Tug & Barge.

In the Victoria Inner Harbour, shortly before eight p.m. on the evening of July 4, 1928, Alphonso Marquis, the cook on the McFarlane Brothers' tug *Restless*, was drying his coat on the stern of another McFarlane tug called *J.W.P.* He was seen doing so by Louis Fointierre, the cook on the *J.W.P.*

Somehow Marquis fell in the water. Two young boys in a rowboat near the Central Wharf, George Edgar and Joseph Hancock, witnessed the fall and called to Ivan for help. With his wife at home five months pregnant with their first child and with little regard for his own life, Ivan jumped into the water fully clothed to aid the struggling Marquis, despite the fact that he was only able to swim a few strokes himself.

With the help of Captain Joseph Barlow of the Island Tug & Barge tug *Hopkins*, and the two boys, Marquis was manhandled onto a scow and taken to the Island Tug & Barge Company dock, where they called the police.

Victoria police constable G. Clare and driver S. Wilkinson responded to the call and for thirty minutes performed artificial respiration and tried using a Pulmotor, a device which forced air into the lungs of Marquis, but to no avail. When the doctor arrived, he pronounced Marquis dead and his remains were subsequently taken away to BC Funeral Parlors.

In modern times, when ordinary people are known to have put their lives on the line to help others, they are called heroes, given certificates of appreciation and have medals placed around their necks. In contrast, Ivan, his clothes and all their contents simply received a good soaking in the harbour.

Just a few months later, in November 1928, Ivan and Beatrice's first child, Beverley (my mother), was born at the Royal Jubilee Hospital in Victoria. She was named after her mother's cousin.

Another major change was in store. After ten years of working on the sea, for reasons that have now passed with time, although it might possibly have been watching Marquis drown, Ivan decided to quit the towboat industry.

Ivan and his first-born, Beverley, enjoy a visit to Shawnigan Lake, around 1929.

This likely shocked his brother-in-law/employer, fellow workers, family and friends alike and his wife, Beatrice, who was more shocked than anyone else. However, he would eventually return to working on the sea in a different capacity.

Ivan then held several jobs and the Clarke family lived in a number of homes in Victoria in the following years. In 1930, he was a proprietor of a magazine shop while his small family moved in with his parents on Blanshard Street. The magazine shop was Ivan's second business venture. The name and location of his shop and how long it lasted have now been lost to time. That same year Ivan and his brother Hugh became master masons, and they would end up lifelong members of the Victoria-Columbia Lodge No. 1, Ancient Free & Accepted Masons in Victoria.

In April 1931, Ivan and Beatrice's son Raymond was born in the Royal Jubilee Hospital. Ivan was working as a salesman for a fruit and produce company, and the family lived on Menzies Street.

Later that year, Ivan became president of Ivan H. Clarke Co., wholesaler of fruit and produce on Blanshard Street, his third business venture. The announcement in the *Daily Colonist* on Sunday, November 15, 1931, on Beverley's third birthday, read as follows:

> **New Wholesale Firm**—formerly with the Independent Fruit Company, Ivan H. Clark and H. B. Porteous have gone into the wholesale fruit and produce business on their own account, occupying temporary premises at the corner of Blanshard and Fisguard [sic] Streets. Both parties comprising the firm, which will be conducted under the name of Ivan H. Clarke, have had considerable experience in the wholesaling of fruit and vegetables, and will carry on with their own capital, independent of all other interests.

Hubert Porteous was actually an accountant at the time. There was a bit of a push then to better organize and monitor the fruit industry as a whole. In the Growers and Shippers Federation proposed by the Independents, the grower would have a real voice in the control over his fruit.

The Clarkes were then living the good life in a nice house in the Fairfield area of Victoria. But hard times hit and Ivan went broke.

He decided to open a grocery store.

Ivan found success in the wholesale fruit and produce business and was able to provide a comfortable life for his family in Victoria. Their prosperity was cut short by the Depression.

Years earlier, his oldest brother, George, had run a grocery store in the Clarkes' old Spring Ridge neighbourhood of Victoria, which he sold to his father's sister Ida and her husband, Will, in 1916. George had then bought Willows Park Grocery in Oak Bay. He had been both grocer and postmaster, and had hired young Ivan and other family members to work in his stores.

With the grocery business in the family background, and after some long chats with George, Ivan went looking for the perfect building to open his store—his fourth business venture. Soon after, he showed Beatrice the inside of his ideal store, and where they would be living in the back of the store in one room with one light bulb and cold running water, as well as outdoor plumbing. Having come from a very comfortable life while Ivan had been working on the tugs, and about to live in primitive conditions in the back of the store, Beatrice said, "No!" and the marriage soon ended. Their daughter, Beverley, was the one who told me about Ivan's grocery store idea but it's uncertain whether or not the store actually materialized.

Separated and at Sea

It was not long after his marriage separation that Ivan leased the store/supply boat *Violet P.*, which was a converted 62-foot fish-packer, and started selling goods along the west coast of Vancouver Island in his fifth business venture. An article in the *Daily Colonist* on February 16, 1932, described what Ivan's store boat meant to the solitary people on the west coast of the island.

FLOATING SHOP WELCOME SIGHT

Craft Regularly Visits Isolated Settlers on West Coast of Island

UCLUELET. Feb 15—Owing to the fact that most travel on the West Coast must be done by boat and as that depends on the mood of the wind and sea, it is hazardous and uncertain. The West Coast offers many surprises to people and one of the strangest things to a visitor is the travelling store which serves the rarely-visited settlers on the coast.

Despite the rough weather and bad gales which rage along this exposed coastline during the Winter months, this little store boat makes regular trips with its welcome supply of fresh foodstuffs from the city. At the Christmas season, although very high seas were running, this little craft came through with the turkeys and other extras for the holiday, even bringing ice cream, much to the delight of many lonely children.

It is not uncommon to see this boat anchored off places where there is but one cabin in the night, waiting for the lonely occupant to row out to the store and do his weekly shopping. One can hardly realize how welcome this little boat is to those lonely settlers as it makes its regular trips back and forth with little regard to the weather. When this little store arrives at such solitary places with its cargo of fresh eggs, butter, fruit, vegetables, meat and confectionery, in addition to a little world news from the city, business is brisk and prices reasonable.

The skipper of this gallant little craft, going into these out-of-the-way places, has made many friends and is able to serve them in numerous ways. He is doing much in making things easier for the pioneers, not only by bringing them the necessities of life, but in breaking the monotony of the winter months on the West Coast.

After his separation from Beatrice, Ivan leased the Violet P. *as a store boat to supply the west coast of Vancouver Island. This was his fifth business venture.* Photo by Stuart Thomson, City of Vancouver Archives, CVA 99-2426

While Ivan was on one of his last trips up the coast on the *Violet P.*, on October 19, 1933, the *Daily Colonist* reported:

> The Violet P. has been making her regular scheduled trips from Victoria to points on the West Coast and return. The Violet P. visits many points of call not made by the ss Princess Norah on the West Coast and is always a very welcome visitor to the more isolated places, bringing foodstuffs from Victoria and anything else required by her customers, making the return trip with whatever freight offers.

Refuge Cove

Refuge Cove, about halfway up the west coast of Vancouver Island, was about to become the site of Ivan's new home.

According to the British Columbia Government Geographical Names Office files, the name Refuge Cove was originally labelled on the British Admiralty Chart 584 in 1861. Captain George Richards of the Royal Navy had surveyed it that year, while he was doing a survey of the west coast of Vancouver Island on HMS *Hecate* for the Admiralty's Hydrographic Office in England. It was so named as it afforded vessels safe anchorage in bad weather. At a latitude of 49°21'42" North (about the same latitude as North Vancouver), and a longitude of 126°16'05" West, Refuge Cove is in the heart of Clayoquot Sound, immediately west of the entrance to Sydney Inlet, just northwest of Flores Island and northwest of Tofino in the Clayoquot Land District.

In the collection of pictures of the late Major George Nicholson, now in the collection of Tofino historian Ken Gibson, is a picture titled *A Scene from Refuge Cove from the 1860s of Sailors from a British Man-of-War Purchasing Salmon from the Indians*. This same picture appears titled as *Monosaht Indians and Sailors from H.M.S. King Fisher at Refuge Cove, 1882* in the book *Mission to Nootka 1874–1900*, edited by Charles Lillard. Either way, this is probably the earliest known picture from Refuge Cove.

The *Daily Colonist* of September 19, 1874, carried an article on the "Mahnohhahsahts" (as spelled in the report) living at Refuge Cove. They were described as "a small…tribe, numbering in all 17," and the report went on to say that "here, as everywhere this season, the run of salmon appears to have been enormous."

"A scene from Refuge Cove from the 1860s of Sailors from a British Man-of-War purchasing salmon from the Indians." This is likely the earliest known photograph from Refuge Cove. Major George Nicholson Collection/Ken Gibson Collection

In *A Directory for the Navigation of the North Pacific Ocean,* first published in 1870, author Alexander George Findlay FRGS writes:

Refuge Cove is just West of Sharp Point and separated from Sydney Inlet by a narrow peninsula. It runs 1½ miles in a N.N.W. direction, is from 1 to 2 cables wide, and affords good anchorage in 4 to 5 fathoms at half a mile within the entrance, well sheltered and secure from all winds, though apparently open to the S.S.E; the entrance, though narrow, is clear of danger... *Canoe Reef,* lying just S.W. of the entrance and three-quarters of a mile westward of Sharp Point, is two feet above high water, but steep-to on the South and West sides. A sailing vessel, if embayed near this part of the coast, would find safety and shelter in Refuge Cove. It can be entered by steering for Sharp Point, bearing N.W. by N. ⅓ N.; pass a cable [about 600 feet/182 metres] West of the point, and then keep close to the eastern shore, and anchor in about 5 fathoms, 7 or 8 cables within the entrance.

From his years in the tugboat industry, as well as his time on the *Violet P.*, Ivan knew a lot about the area when he decided to set in motion his plan to move there. Having made up his mind to start a new, land-based enterprise at Refuge Cove, he borrowed around a thousand dollars from his mother and an undisclosed financial backer, whom in later years Ivan discreetly disclosed to a few family members, including my mother, as being long-time family friend Allan D. Ballantyne, president of Ballantyne Brothers and also a florist on Fort Street (and later on Douglas Street) in Victoria. One of my first recollections of my mother talking about her father when I was a very young boy was when she pointed out Ballantyne's store on lower Douglas Street, telling me the owner of the flower store was the man who grubstaked her father to help start up his store on Vancouver Island's west coast.

Ivan visited the Land Registry office in Victoria to see what land, if any, was available at Refuge Cove. In early March 1933, he boarded the BC Coast Service 250-foot 1-inch SS *Princess Norah* in Victoria to head up the west coast and disembark at Tofino, where he hired a boat and headed out to Refuge Cove on a scouting mission. Not having enough capital money to set himself up with a store and pay in full for land, when he got back to Victoria he again went to the Land Registry office to apply for a Crown Land Grant on Clayoquot Land District Lots 1371 and 1372, as mentioned in chapter 1.

By the fall of 1933, Ivan had secured mail-order accounts with the Victoria wholesalers Wilson Brothers Wholesale Grocers, Kelly Douglas & Co., McDonalds Consolidated and W. H. Malkin Co. He then purchased his initial grocery stock and merchandise and made his way back up the coast. As indicated earlier, he arrived with his two dogs on the BC Coast Service 233-foot 7-inch SS *Princess Maquinna* at the Gibson Brothers' wharf at Matilda Creek, in Matilda Inlet, near Ahousat on Flores Island, and then made his way with the Ahousaht people's help to Refuge Cove.

The *Maquinna* had just replaced the *Norah*, which had been temporarily relieving the former on the west coast run. The *Maquinna* had been built in Esquimalt in 1913 for about $300,000, and ran up and down the west coast of Vancouver Island. The ship had been given the nickname "Old Faithful." For many years, about every ten days, the ship steamed the almost 850-mile (1,360-km) round-trip voyage from Victoria to Port Alice with a schedule of about 45 stops servicing logging shows, Indigenous villages, canneries,

Ivan, standing at left, opened his Refuge Cove general store in the fall of 1933. Two-year-old Raymond is pictured leaning against the tree, next to Ivan's dog. Hugh S. Clarke Collection

fishing camps, mining camps and west coast ports. About half of those were regular scheduled stops.

The loss of his collie dog to a cougar failed to slow Ivan down and his remote general store proved immediately popular.

That summer, the *Daily Colonist* reported that cougars were "exceptionally plentiful" on Vancouver Island's west coast. It was also reported that there was a significant decrease in the deer population due to an unknown liver disease, as well as other wildlife that the cougars relied on for food. This might explain the sudden change in diet for the now starving cougars, who were desperate enough to begin raiding chicken houses, killing family pets and stalking children. In Ucluelet, one mother found a cougar bold enough to stalk her children within 6 metres of the house. Thankfully, she was able to get all her children safely inside the house, but after that cougar was killed they discovered a coat with four buttons still attached to it in the cougar's stomach. The following summer, it was noted that there was also an increased number of bears on the west coast of Vancouver Island, and that cougars were still causing damage and loss of property at many points. That summer, seven cougars had been killed in just a few weeks on a local reserve.

Ivan's store would quickly become the local general store for boats of all shapes and sizes anchored in the cove as well as for the surrounding communities including Estevan Point, Boat Basin and Hesquiat Harbour. Ivan also served people who were timber cruising and logging in and around Sydney Inlet, as well as prospectors hoping to stake a claim on a copper mine motherlode and other minerals. It's interesting that Ivan would live in copper mine country, just as his father had while growing up in Bruce Mines, Ontario. In 1862 Ivan's grandfather George Clark discovered a vein of copper while moving his cattle. One of his cows slipped on a rock, overturning the moss that covered the vein. The discovery became the Wellington Copper Mine. George sold his claim to the Montréal mining company for the price of a Y2 barrel of salt pork, a barrel of flour, ten dollars and a job for $1.25 a day as long as the mine remained open.

Ivan thus became the first permanent non-Indigenous person living in Refuge Cove. Prior to his arrival, there was a handful of tumbledown shacks on the opposite shore occupied only in the fall months by a few Nuu-chah-nulth families.

During the summer of 1933 a large-scale marine survey of Refuge Cove had been completed by the hydrographic survey ship *William J. Stewart*, named after the revered Canadian Dominion hydrographer. Refuge Cove was officially labelled on British Admiralty Charts on April 3, 1934, not long after Ivan arrived. The 214-foot ss *William J. Stewart* was built in Collingwood, Ontario, for the Canadian government Department of Marine and Fisheries in 1932, and was based out of Victoria. The ship was the last reciprocating steam engine-powered vessel of its type in British Columbia. After its retirement in 1979, it was renamed the *Canadian Princess* and towed to Ucluelet, where it became very much a tourist attraction, used as a floating fishing resort. On September 30, 2016, the ship was towed from its mooring in Ucluelet's harbour by the 54-foot 5-inch tug *Island Sentry* to Amix Salvage in Surrey, BC, to be dismantled.

End of a Marriage

In the Supreme Court of British Columbia in Victoria on December 14, 1933, Justice Fisher presided over the trial for the divorce of Ivan and Beatrice. No one appeared for the respondent (Ivan was at Refuge Cove by then), and Mr.

Henry E. A. Courtney appeared for the petitioner (Beatrice). Mr. Patrick J. P. Sinnott, Ivan's solicitor, did send a letter on Ivan's behalf.

Justice Fisher quickly ruled that the marriage between Ivan and Beatrice "was hereby absolutely dissolved as from this date by reason that since the solemnization thereof the said Respondent has been guilty of adultery." At that time, if one or the other admitted to adultery, even though it did not

After his parents divorced, Raymond came to live with Ivan at Refuge Cove. Father and son are shown in their travelling clothes aboard the Maquinna *on their way to the cove.*

actually happen, the process of getting a divorce was quick and easy, without going through a lengthy trial. In doing so, Ivan had made it easy for Beatrice to get the divorce.

The court further ordered that the couple's two children, Beverley and Raymond, remain in the "absolute custody, possession and control" of their mother, provided their father "shall have reasonable access to the said children at such times and places as shall be agreed upon by the Petitioner and the Respondent, and with liberty to either party to apply for directions concerning such access should he or she be advised." It was not until more recent years that the tables turned and it became common for fathers to be granted partial or full custody of their children after a divorce. The court further ordered that Ivan pay Beatrice's "cost of this action forthwith after taxation." Ivan was not ordered to pay alimony or child support.

Times were tough in the early 1930s when Ivan and Beatrice divorced. Beatrice did not have the means to care for both of the children on her own, so sadly they were separated. Beverley went with her mom to live with her McDonald grandparents and Ivan took Raymond. Raymond appears in the only known picture of Ivan's large canvas tent trading post/general store at Refuge Cove, next to Ivan's Airedale, which suggests that Raymond had probably gone up to Refuge Cove with his dad that first autumn.

Front Page News in 1934

Over the years that Ivan was at the cove, more than two dozen newspaper articles were written about him and the hot springs, and he was mentioned in many more, as well as in his former rum-running friend and author Major George Nicholson's book, *Vancouver Island's West Coast 1762–1962*, all of which helped bring Ivan and the hot springs to the attention of the general public.

In 1934 Ivan made his first appearance in a BC directory. Using information that could have been gathered up to a year earlier, the 1934 Sun British Columbia Directory included the following information in its entry for nearby Riley's Cove, on the northeast tip of Flores Island: "A landing in Sydney Inlet on West Coast of Vancouver Island. Served by CPR Steamers. Ahousat 15 mile east, is nearest post office." Residents for the entire area were listed as Ivan Clarke, "Fish Buyer"; Ispaco Fish Packers Ltd. Oils and Meals; Harold

Johnson, "Chemist"; Robert Ogden, "General Contractor (East Bay)"; and George Rae-Arthur, "Carpenter." Johnson was probably working at Ispaco, Ogden at nearby East Bay and Rae-Arthur was more than likely helping Ivan at Refuge Cove.

The first big newspaper article written about Ivan at Refuge Cove started with a banner across the top of the front page of the *Daily Colonist* on Thursday, September 20, 1934, exclaiming: "Develops Hot Springs—Refuge Cove on West Coast May Become a New Health Resort—Page 10." The article itself read:

To Develop Hot Springs
Victorians Locate at Refuge Cove on West Coast of Island

Refuge Cove, Sept. 19.—A new port of call for the steamers of the CPR West Coast service was formally inaugurated by the SS Princess Norah on her last north bound trip, when she called at the hot springs, Refuge Cove, landing passengers, supplies and household effects.

Ivan H. Clark [*sic*], of Victoria has established a general store and fish buying camp at this point, which he operated during the past summer. It was for the purpose of landing his Winter supplies that the Princess Norah made the call. It is Mr. Clark's intention to further develop the hot springs and eventually establish a resort there. Captain R. W. McMurray, general manager of the BC Coast Service has agreed to include Refuge Cove as a stopping place for the West Coast steamers as business offers. The passengers disembarking this trip were Ivan Clark, returning from a business trip to Victoria, Mrs. W. H. Clark, Master Clark and Miss M. Stevens [actually "Stephen," mentioned further in chapter 4], who is spending a vacation there.

SNUG HARBOR

While Refuge Cove is new as a port of call for the regular West Coast passenger steamers, it is a well-known harbor to all fishing boats and vessels in the service of the Marine and Fisheries Departments.

Situated just beyond the entrance to Sidney Inlet, the Cove, which in reality is a well-sheltered and snug harbor two miles long, deep water, has good anchorage in all weather and is easy of access to the ocean. Practically all of the fishing boats, halibut, salmon and pilchard engaged in fishing off of Sidney Inlet and Estevan make Refuge Cove their headquarters during the summer months and take refuge there in bad weather.

It is here in Refuge Cove that the little known West Coast hot sulphur springs are located, being off the "beaten track" of travelers; but for many years well-known and much patronized by all engaged in the fishing industry of the West Coast. Scarcely a fisherman passes up or down the West Coast but stops at the springs for a bath.

SHOWER BATH

The springs are uniquely situated on the rocky shoreline at the entrance to the Cove, the main spring, which in reality is a flow of water at almost the boiling point to the extent of several thousand gallons per minute, emerging from a deep fissure in the rock at a point about two hundred feet from the high tide mark, and from here it flows in the form of a small stream down towards the sea, finally creating a waterfall about ten feet high and under which a half-a-dozen persons can easily stand to enjoy the shower. At this point the water is still exceedingly hot, being about the temperature of an exceptionally hot bath, the flow still being several thousand gallons per minute. The fall ends in a large pool in the rocks below, and at high tide one may enjoy the novelty of actually getting a warm bath, the hot water mingling with the salt water of the Pacific Ocean during the few hours of high tide.

The second big newspaper article about Ivan at Refuge Cove was written by Ruth Cooper, and was printed in the *Daily Colonist* on Sunday, October 28, 1934, just over a month after his first major newspaper write-up.

Titled "Refuge Cove Hot Springs Give Health and Pleasure," Cooper's article was about an earlier trip she had taken with her husband to Refuge Cove looking for the elusive hot springs. She knew only that the hot springs were on the west coast of Vancouver Island, while her husband, Robert knew the location but only surmised the way to get there. They set out prepared to be isolated for two or three weeks.

According to the article, the Coopers took the train to Port Alberni and then boarded the *Princess Norah* to make their way to Riley's Cove on Flores Island. The *Norah* was running late and at two a.m. the steward came to their room and said that the captain wanted to leave in an hour's time and that breakfast was waiting for them. They dressed, hurriedly consumed breakfast and scrambled ashore. They foraged around but found no place to sleep other than the wharf. So they made the best of it and settled down to a very imaginative and eerie night. The story of the cougar making off with Ivan's collie and other cougar stories were now folklore material. The Coopers had heard all about them on the trip up the coast on the *Norah*. They spent the rest of the night on the wharf listening to every sound and watching every tree move, imagining it was a marauding cougar stealthily coming to make off with their own dog, which they had actually brought for their protection, but now it was the dog who needed theirs.

The couple awoke to a glorious sunrise, and people were very surprised to see them on the wharf so early in the morning. Laura Henshall, the wife of the postmaster, sent their son David down to invite them for breakfast. After breakfast, they were given a much-appreciated ride in a gas-powered boat across the water to the Ahousaht First Nation's reserve at Swans Cove on the east side of Openit Peninsula. They tramped through the woods for what seemed like a mile across the peninsula to Refuge Cove and were very surprised to find cheery Ivan Clarke set up there with his log cabin and fully stocked store.

The Coopers' original plan was to pack everything out to the hot springs, but after weighing the pros and cons of trying to take everything by canoe, along with the difficulties of landing near the hot springs, or by personally packing them out, they decided to set up camp at Ivan's, and they picked a spot overlooking the bay.

Determined to make them as comfortable as possible, Ivan helped to rig their tent and lent them a camp stove, as well as his canoe and his rowboat. Luckily for the Coopers, a man who was working for Ivan paddled his canoe around to Swan Cove on the other side and picked up their baggage and provisions, so they did not have to make several trips back across the peninsula to fetch their belongings. The man was more than likely George Rae-Arthur. At that time, Ivan told Ruth Cooper that she was the first non-Indigenous woman to camp there, so her trip must have been previous to Ivan's mother permanently moving to the cove. It went through Ruth's mind after the trek to Refuge Cove that she might be the first Caucasian woman to be buried there.

The first time the visitors hiked the primitive trail out to the hot springs, they scrambled over, under, and across logs and over huge ravines. The banks were particularly challenging to climb up with only roots as handholds. Although it was hard work, they enjoyed the exercise.

The Coopers heated their lunch of canned soup by depositing it in the hot water coming out of the rocks. Down by the pools among the rocks they found caches of soap left behind by passing fishermen. Ruth mentioned how exhilarating it was for them after taking their hot bath to dash into the cold salt water. Given the slipperiness of the rocky shoreline, there likely wasn't a whole lot of dashing going on. They even drank plenty of the sulphur water, which she said was not so strong as to be obnoxious. Canada was in the depths of the Depression, and being a city lady, Ruth even thought about the boon it would be in times to come for people who could not afford the high prices connected with hydro to be able to bathe in the hot springs.

She said the cove was full of endless surprises and mentioned the many activities there were, such as trout fishing in the small stream at the end of the inlet, more trout fishing in a small lake about half a mile up that stream, as well as trolling for salmon at the mouth of the cove. For hunters there was plenty of game such as small birds, cougars, bears and deer. One could explore the small rocky islands with pools that formed natural aquariums filled with all manner of amphibians. There were ferns to study on the trees—some 10 to 12 feet (3–3.7 m) high and four feet (1.2 m) thick—and wild blueberries were in abundance.

At five o'clock each evening, Japanese fishing boats would come in from the outside to unload their fish at Ivan's cold storage, disturbing the quiet peace of the cove with the chugging of their engines. One night, there had been a stiff wind blowing and numerous boats came in to seek shelter in the cove, but by morning they were all gone. Ruth said great credit must be given to Ivan as he had lived up there alone in a tent the past winter until he cleared a spot and built his log cabin. According to her, by the time she and her husband arrived, Ivan had logged about an acre (0.4 hectares) of land and had planted some potatoes. He had also built a long float with a storage house for fish and another for gasoline on the end of it. The following winter he had plans to reconstruct the trail to the hot springs by shortening it and making it easier to travel over. He also wanted to build several cabins, which he would rent out for a moderate sum.

CHAPTER 4

Marriage Aboard *Maquinna*:
New Start at the Cove

I van became engaged to Mary Isobel "Mabel" Stephen the year after the second newspaper article appeared about his life at Refuge Cove. Ivan and Mabel had grown up in the same part of Victoria and she was living with her parents there when he sent for her to join him at Refuge Cove. They were married aboard the *Princess Maquinna* in January 1935 on what turned out to be an extremely wintry day.

On Monday, January 7, 1935, in Victoria, thirty-year-old Mabel attended the Women's Benefit Association local review, Queen Alexandra Review No. 1, where the new officers for 1935 were installed. Prior to the installation of officers, a business meeting was held at which three applications for new members were received. After the financial report was read, the review extended best wishes to Mabel, who was leaving that week for the west coast.

A few days later, on the evening of Friday, January 11, Mabel boarded the BC Coast Service SS *Princess Maquinna* by the old-fashioned gangplank at dock level. Her family and friends were permitted to roam the ship at will until about five minutes before sailing. At about 11 p.m., the *Maquinna* pulled away from her inside berth at the Canadian Pacific Steamship dock on Belleville Street in Victoria for west coast points. The trip north to Ahousat would have cost her about $10.50, which would have included her stateroom and all of her meals, starting with a free midnight supper. Afternoon tea was also free. A stewardess took care of the female passengers as well as the children on board.

The *Maquinna* had about twenty-six northbound scheduled stops, with Port Renfrew being the first and then Clo-oose and Bamfield, as well as miscellaneous logging camps, canneries and fish reduction plants along Barkley Sound until they reached Port Alberni, where the passengers had several hours ashore. On the second day, there were ports of call at Ucluelet, Tofino, Clayoquot and Kakawis before Mabel arrived at Matilda Creek.

Ivan couldn't have picked a worse day to get married. The west coast of Vancouver Island had been hit hard by zero-degree weather and heavy snow. As the *Maquinna* only stopped at Refuge Cove when there was cargo to drop off, and because there wasn't a minister at the cove, Ivan had to take his gas-powered freight boat to Matilda Creek, on the west side of Matilda Inlet, to meet the *Maquinna*. With his suit safely packed in his suitcase, Ivan stowed his luggage away as best he could, probably covered in a tarpaulin for added protection in his open boat. In the freezing cold with poor visibility in the blowing snow, it would have been a very miserable trip down to Matilda Creek. In the early evening of Sunday, January 13, the *Maquinna* would have tied up at the old Gibson Brothers' wharf at Matilda Creek.

On that Sunday in 1935, aboard the *Princess Maquinna*, docked at Matilda Creek, just north of the village of Ahousat, Ivan was married for his second time.

Reverend Joseph Jones of the Ahousaht Presbyterian Mission did the honours at Ivan and Mabel's wedding. The master of the *Maquinna*, William Thompson, gave the bride away. Witnesses were Mary Livesley of Ahousat and Donald MacRaild from Victoria, who was the chief engineer on the *Maquinna*.

The *Maquinna* more than likely remained tied up to the old Gibson wharf for the night, and Ivan and Mabel would have reserved Mabel's stateroom for their first night together. Unfortunately, it would have been a short night, as the *Maquinna* would have backed away from the wharf very early the next morning.

Although Mabel and Ivan had lived in the same area of Victoria while growing up, she had gone to the old Kings Road school and Ivan had gone to Spring Ridge School, and then Hillside School. Afterwards, though, they

Ivan and Mabel were married aboard the Maquinna *on January 13, 1935. They made their home together in Refuge Cove until Mabel's death in 1964. Their daughter Patsy would remember Mabel as "the work shoes and brains of the factory, she was the one that kept the place going."* Major George Nicholson Collection/Ken Gibson Collection

went to high school together. While living with her parents, she had been working as a salesperson for Stevenson's Chocolates just before leaving Victoria. By coincidence, at that time, Beatrice Clarke was working at the nearby Peggy Page Chocolates, formerly the world-famous 'Barrington Chocolates' owned by chocolatier Emily Barrington Elworthy, Harold's only sister.

Log Cabin

Within a few months of arriving at Refuge Cove in 1933, Ivan had built a log cabin about 16 feet by 16 feet (5×5 m), using 6- to 10-inch (15–25-cm) diameter logs, and then a long float, using larger logs, more than likely with the help of George Rae-Arthur. By November 1934, he had built a wood-framed addition on the north side of the log cabin and an enclosed lean-to on the back of it. He had felled about twenty large trees and many smaller ones to open up a rough clearing around his store, which would have supplied him with the logs to build his cabin, logs to build his float and a supply of firewood to last a very long time.

The following year he built a store and two wood-frame houses, one for him and Mabel and one for his mother, Annie Emma Clarke. Annie Emma

Business at Ivan's general store was good, and within a matter of months he built a log cabin to replace his canvas tent. Major George Nicholson Collection/Ken Gibson Collection

had followed Ivan to Refuge Cove soon after his arrival. At age 75, having been widowed in 1931, finished with raising her own children and being from tough pioneer stock, she moved to Refuge Cove to raise her twenty-fifth grandchild, Raymond, and to make sure Ivan did not waste the money that she had lent to him. In a July 1934 letter to her granddaughter, Beverley Clarke (Ray's sister), Annie Emma mentions how dangerous it was for small children at Refuge Cove. She tells of how Raymond stayed away from the banks, because if he fell over he would be badly hurt among the large rocks and boulders.

To build the store and two houses in 1935, Ivan used lumber he salvaged from an abandoned copper mine at the mouth of a creek at the end of Stewardson Inlet, an arm off nearby Sydney Inlet, and he also salvaged some from abandoned buildings at Riley's Cove, 6 miles (9.6 km) away, by boat. Out of necessity, having little capital, Ivan had gone "green," recycling building materials and other supplies, many years before it became the popular thing to do. Afterwards, he added to the original main building at irregular intervals.

Backing onto Ivan's Lot 1372 was the 77-acre (190-hectare) Ahousaht First Nation Openit No. 27 Reserve established in 1889, with water frontage on

Ivan's mother, Annie Emma, moved to Refuge Cove at the age of seventy-five to raise Raymond, her twenty-fifth grandchild. The wood-frame home that Ivan built for her was constructed using salvaged materials. The repurposing of building supplies would prove to be a constant feature of life at Refuge Cove.

Swan Cove on the western shore of Sydney Inlet. By this time Robert Wyllie, a commercial agent for Canada Overseas Agency and the son of an international merchant/importer, owned the southern lot on Openit Peninsula containing the hot springs. Up to at least the early 1920s, the springs had been referred to as Sharp Point Hot Springs. Sometime after that they became known as Ramsay Hot Springs, possibly named after Robert's wife, the former Eloise Mae Ramsey (note the two spellings). Ramsay Hot Springs was first recorded in the 1953 BC Gazetteer and formally adopted on December 31, 1966, on 92E/8 as listed in 1966 BC Gazetteer. The origin/significance of the name had not been recorded.

A *Daily Colonist* article written by Ivan's good friend, Major George Nicholson, described the hot springs as "being at the extreme tip of a wooded promontory on what may well be described as the most exposed part of Vancouver Island's west coast." The only way to get to the hot springs by foot was by crossing Ivan's property, unless you happened upon them in a small craft on a calm day at high tide and you could beach your boat on the rocky shore, but that didn't happen very often and beaching a boat there is a tricky manoeuvre in itself.

When Ivan arrived, Refuge Cove was a very remote place known only to nearby Indigenous inhabitants and to sailors, fishermen, prospectors and the few others with boats whose livelihoods took them up the west coast of the island. The hot springs at the southeast corner of the cove were the only major ones on Vancouver Island, though there are eight other marine hot springs on the coast of British Columbia, including smaller hot springs at Ahousat that are not as hot or deep, and some farther north in Haida Gwaii's National Park.

In the beginning, there was no direct steamship service to Refuge Cove. Ivan had to use his gas-powered freight boat or paddle his canoe to Riley's Cove to pick up his general store supplies and mail. If the timing was right, sometimes George Nicholson would tow him there with his 35-foot 5-inch troller/work boat *Miowera* when he was coming down from his home in Zeballos. If the weather was lousy, Ivan paddled his canoe up the cove to a trail, hiked across Openit Peninsula, took another canoe that he had stored and paddled it across to Riley's Cove. Both ends of this trail were situated in smaller coves and Ivan gave them both the same whimsical name, "God's Pocket," because they shortened the distance he needed to portage his load.

Ivan reversed the trip laden with his supplies and had to carry them back across the trail, making as many trips back and forth as necessary, and then paddled his supplies down to his store. As his son Hugh said in an interview many years ago, "In the early days, he had lots of time on his hands to make trips like that."

Annual precipitation at the cove is very heavy, estimated at about 120–150 inches (300–375 cm) a year, mainly falling from October to March. There was a stream that ran right beside the store, which Ivan dammed and used for his fresh water supply. He eventually dug a well, about 10 feet (3 m) deep, which he lined with wood. Later on, he had a water tower built on the hill behind the store, which he pumped the well water up into to supply his home and business. Ivan's son Hugh remembered always having running water in their house. This part of the west coast of Vancouver Island has some of the best drinking water in British Columbia.

Business Starts to Grow

The cove was situated centrally to good fishing grounds, containing— depending on the time of year—sockeye, coho, pink, chum and spring salmon as well as winter steelhead, pilchard and herring. So, almost at the start, Ivan decided to expand his business and set up a fish-buying camp to save the fishermen the 40-mile (64-km) return trip north to Nootka or south to Tofino. They were quick to take advantage of this new service. The larger fish companies followed suit and soon had their own fish-buying camps in the cove.

Before telephones arrived, all outside communication at the cove was done through Ivan by the newly installed government telegraph service. Telegraph operation was something he had learned during his tugboat days. As soon as he was able to, Ivan had applied to the Dominion government Telegraph Service in Ottawa for a connection to the Alberni-Clayoquot telegraph line, and then had to wait for their reply and hope his request had been granted. It was not long until Ivan was appointed government telegraph agent for Refuge Cove, which meant he had to be around to receive or send telegraphs, carefully recording in a ledger all incoming and outgoing telegraphs, along with the costs. He would have also been responsible for delivering any telegraphs within a certain radius, but in reality, unless it was an emergency he probably held any incoming telegraphs until the recipient's next visit to his store.

Toward the end of May 1935, Herbert E. Elsden of the Government Telegraph Service spent some time with Ivan and Mabel at Refuge Cove upgrading the telegraph wiring and equipment in his store. Ivan's white-on-dark-blue porcelain "Govt Telegraph Office" sign now hangs in his son Hugh's store at Ahousat.

In other communications developments, Riley's Cove postmaster and machinist George R. Henshall resigned his postmaster position on September 25, 1935, also leaving his job running the fish oil–refining plant along with his logging operation. John B. Hardinge only temporarily filled in the postmaster position, which left an opportunity for Ivan to look into starting a post office at Refuge Cove.

On July 21, 1936, Ivan became postmaster of the Sydney Inlet Post Office, which he opened up in his store located on Clayoquot Land District Lot 1372, quite possibly being sworn in by William Thompson, the master of the *Maquinna*. It's uncertain what Ivan's sales pitch was to the post office superintendent in Ottawa, as he certainly did not have the population in the cove to warrant a post office, but he probably used the number of fishermen that now regularly used the cove as his argument to open one. From 1917 to 1927 there had been a Sydney Inlet Post Office and store run by Lawrence W. Carter at the Indian Chief Mine, owned by the Tidewater Copper Co. Ltd., in nearby Stewardson Inlet.

Ivan's duty as postmaster by definition of the Supreme Court of Canada was "to take charge of his post office, to collect, safeguard and account for the revenue of the office, to hire, supervise and control any staff and issue such instructions as might be necessary to secure prompt and expeditious handling of mail, to deal with complaints concerning the service given by the office and make adjustments when found desirable or necessary and to perform other related work as required."

Hiring, supervising and controlling staff was made easy by having family members help out. There was no sense in complaining about the time it took for letters to be sent or to arrive, as until the mail was brought in and taken out by air, the mail schedule was governed by the day that the *Maquinna* arrived, which was about every ten days. If the expected mail did not arrive on that "boat day," locals would just have to wait until the next one.

I AM DRAWING YOU A BOAT

As postmaster of the Sydney Inlet Post Office, Ivan oversaw the collection and distribution of all mail in Refuge Cove, including letters from his family. Beverley Clarke mailed this drawing of a boat to Ivan in February 1936.

In the beginning, his remuneration as postmaster came primarily from the sale of postage stamps and money-order commissions from his customers rather than a salary. Ivan would hold the postmaster position until May 22, 1968.

A Birth and a Death

At Refuge Cove in early November 1936, Mabel Clarke, well into her third trimester of her first pregnancy, was helped aboard the southbound *Maquinna* from the big freight boat. She was heading down to Victoria to stay with her parents until her baby was born. She returned on the northbound *Maquinna* in the middle of December, bringing home her first child, born in early December, whom Ivan and Mabel named Hugh Stephen.

After Hugh's birth, Ivan, Mabel and their small family had only been back home at the cove for just over two weeks when in late December 1936 his brother-in-law, Captain Jim Olson, was stricken with a heart attack and dropped dead on the deck of his ship, the 1914 58-foot tug *Fairbanks*, while it was approaching the dock in Bellingham, Washington. It had been towing a barge of cross-arms. At that time, the *Fairbanks* was being operated by the Port Renfrew logging company Hemmingsen and Cameron.

Not long after Ivan had obtained his Master's Certificate, Captain Jim Olson had retired, but like most mariners could not stay away from the sea and eventually was back on the water again. Jim fulfilled different jobs on local tugs until he was offered the skipper's position on the *Fairbanks*. When Jim's former longtime employer, Captain George McGregor, owner of the Victoria Tug Company, heard of Jim's sudden passing, he said Jim was one of the most well-known skippers in the tugboat business on the coast, and he personally regretted to hear of his recent death.

The following newspaper article appeared in the Victoria *Daily Times* after Jim Olson's funeral:

CAPT. J.F. OLSON

Many sorrowing friends attended the funeral of Captain James Ferdinand Olson, held Thursday afternoon. Rev. W. G. Wilson, D.D., conducting the service, during which the hymns, "Nearer My God to Thee" and "Jesus, Saviour, Pilot Me," were sung. The casket and hearse were banked with beautiful floral tributes. The following acted as pallbearers: R.L. Clarke, Axel Olson, Oscar Olson, Oscar Molin, Mr. Davidson and Capt. M. Matheson. The remains were laid at rest in Royal Oak Burial Park.

Improvements Noticed

As life continued at the cove, an article appeared in the *Daily Colonist* under the heading "All Business Shows Market Recovery on Island's West Coast." Written out of Ucluelet on January 4, 1937, it included the following paragraph.

Among other smaller developments of public interest on the West Coast during 1936 was the improvements made of the natural mineral springs at Refuge Cove. It is anticipated that these mineral baths will become very popular when completely expanded and made more accessible to visitors. They are expected to become a great attraction to the West Coast when thoroughly advertised.

Despite newspaper reports to the contrary, the hot springs themselves remained largely undeveloped in the late 1930s. Visitor access was improving, however, thanks to enhancements to Ivan's float at Refuge Cove (shown here with the 112-foot RCMP vessel Adversus) and the trail out to the springs.

The wording of the article probably originated from Ivan himself. In reality, nothing had been happening out at the hot springs themselves other than that Ivan had been improving the trail to them. The improvements were his buildings and float at Clayoquot Land District Lot 1372 where his now three-year-old business was slowly being developed. The float gave people a place to safely dock their boats, where they could then start their hike out to the springs. Not having an advertising budget per se, as always word of mouth and any newspaper print he could obtain was free advertising for Ivan.

The post office also got attention when the British Columbia and Yukon Directory listed it for the first time in 1937. It was noted as being in Sydney Inlet, though, when it was actually in Refuge Cove. It was described as "a Post Office on the west coast of Vancouver Island, 25 miles north of Clayoquot, in Alberni-Nanaimo Provincial Electoral District reached by CPR boats from Victoria." Documented inhabitants included "Canadian Government Postmaster—I.H. Clarke." Ivan appears in a second entry as "Clarke Ivan H., Fish

Boardwalks were another early improvement at Refuge Cove. Raymond (standing),
Hugh and a canine friend enjoy some sunshine on the path to Annie Emma's cottage,
built by Ivan in 1935.

Buyer and P.M.," along with his brother Ralph and their mother. The list also included five fishermen and one "Fisherman and Trapper."

Ivan became harbour master in 1937, the year in which the *Maquinna* started to make Refuge Cove a regular port of call, even though there were still no proper facilities to dock the ship. The Dominion government eventually provided a wharf.

When Refuge Cove became a designated harbour, and when the Dominion of Canada finally built a wharf, the Dominion government minister of transport hired Ivan for both the harbour master and wharfinger positions. He was not a Transport Canada employee, but rather a part-time "fees of office" ministerial appointee. His remuneration each year would have been based on the size of his wharf and the number of vessels coming and going.

As harbour master and wharfinger, he would have been responsible for monitoring marine activities in the harbour. According to the Government of Canada, he would have also been responsible for "monitoring and directing the use of the wharf, and for assessing appropriate berthage, wharfage, storage and other fees under the *Canada Marine Act*," making sure that appropriate fees were paid. As well he would have served as the "eyes and ears" for Transport Canada's regional office, keeping an eye on

Visitors to Refuge Cove in the late 1930s were greeted by Ivan's store (centre), flanked by his storage shed (left) and house.

the community and offering up local knowledge when needed. At about the same time, Ivan had painted, in crude hand lettering and with a big arrow pointing to the south, "Trail to Hot Springs" on the front of his tool shed overlooking the cove for all to see from the water. He also had a big sign with "STORE" professionally painted in white letters mounted on the roof above the porch on the front of his store.

By 1940, close to two hundred salmon trawlers used Refuge Cove as their base during the eight-month-long fishing season, as did some seine boats. Many moved away when peak fish runs happened in other parts of the coast, but for the greater part of the fishing season they used Refuge Cove as their home port.

Government Discusses Spas

In Vancouver on November 16, 1943, Dr. Arthur W. Paskins announced that a token gift of $25,000 had been given to the University of British Columbia by an "industrialist" to establish a Chair of Physical Medicine at the university. Dr. Paskins was a naturopathic physician in BC, and had been the director of the Associated Nature Cure & Physiotherapy Institute during the 1920s and '30s.

The expectation was that the provincial and federal governments would also need to make similar contributions to help finance the new university department and the related health spas, which could easily rise to several million dollars. The unknown patron stood ready to invest "unlimited funds" for the establishment of a series of health spas at selected hot springs in the province.

The subject of spas and medicinal clays and earth had been comprehensively dealt with in the Legislature several years earlier. At that time, the hot springs on the west coast of Vancouver Island were mentioned as one of the possible locations. The hot springs at Refuge Cove were certainly not perking to the surface through medicinal clays. They rose through bedrock and flowed down to the ocean over a stony base stream and rock outcroppings.

Certainly, if the government informant of the day had actually taken the time to look at the Ramsay Hot Springs, that location would quickly have been deemed an unsuitable candidate for a university-run medicinal clay and earth health spa.

Killer Whales Stranded

The death of a killer whale in the waters of British Columbia makes front-page news in our time. In more recent past years, whale beachings seemed to be more frequently heard of on the east coast of Canada and the United States than on this coast. On June 12, 1945, though, thirteen killer whales accidently beached themselves between Boulder Point and Estevan Point, not far from Ivan's operation in Refuge Cove. They were found the next day by Noah Paul from the Hesquiaht First Nation village. Sadly none of the whales survived and word did not get back to the scientific community for almost two weeks.

This beach has a gentle slope and contains very little sand or gravel. Instead, large boulders worn smooth by water action are strewn along the shore. These boulders can be seen in the picture of the stranded barge in the same area, on page 79 of this book. When all the evidence was accumulated, the theory from the scientific community was that it was an accidental beaching during the falling tide while the whales were in the shallow waters in the pursuit of prey.

When director George Clifford Carl of the British Columbia Provincial Museum of Natural History and Anthropology presented his March 1946 report on the museum's 1945 activities, Ivan and Mabel Clarke were among those thanked for all their assistance during the study of the whale carcasses.

There had been other instances of mass killer whale beachings in the years leading up to the 1945 event. In January 1941, eleven adult killer whales were stranded on another gradually inclining beach near Masset, Queen Charlotte Island (Haida Gwaii). A couple of years later, a number of killer whales were again stranded on a beach near Cherry Point on Vancouver Island. This group managed to escape, with the only casualty being one newborn female who had been trapped in a slight depression.

CHAPTER 5

Sydney Inlet School:
Meeting a Big Family's Needs

I f all of Ivan and Mabel's children had been of school age at the same time, there would have been enough Clarkes to fulfill the requirements for a government teacher at Refuge Cove. They had eight children born between 1936 and 1946: Hugh, Nada, William (Billy), Arthur (Art), Patricia (Patsy), James (Jimmy), Ivan (Buddy) and Diane. All were born in Victoria except for Buddy, who was born in Tofino.

In those years, according to the Ministry of Education policies, there needed to be seven students before the government would pay the salary for a teacher. The communities themselves had to provide the schoolhouses.

Ivan's son from his first marriage, Raymond, had started out being educated by his grandmother at the cove. She mentioned in a letter to Ray's sister, Beverley, in February 1937, that Ray was doing his best to print a letter to send to his mother, but she wanted Ray to learn to write, and she would sit down with Ray and teach him a little each evening after tea. She once again mentioned that Ray had not been outside to play since they had returned to the cove and reiterated that it had been too slippery and dangerous to let him out alone. She finished by telling Beverley that one of her aunties had seen her at a concert at the Empress Hotel in Victoria and said how nice she looked and what a big girl she was getting to be. Over the years, Raymond and his grandmother went back and forth to Victoria to visit.

Hugh and Nada were sent to Victoria to live with their Stephen grandparents and to attend school before there were enough students to fill the quota at Refuge Cove. Hugh remembers going to Victoria for Grades 1 and 2 at the old North Ward School where his mom had also gone.

When enough of their children reached school age, it was time for Ivan and Mabel to provide a school for them. The alternative was to send all the children to live with their Stephen grandparents, since by then school had become mandatory in British Columbia.

Schoolhouse, Teacher

In about 1945, the Gibson family was closing down the last of their operation at Matilda Creek, as they were in the process of building a new sawmill at Tahsis. Their Matilda Creek operation had consisted of two fish reduction plant buildings that ran seasonally, a small sawmill and shingle mill. Of the nine buildings they had for sale, Ivan purchased four of them. The land just above the foreshore at the cove was more or less cleared for each of the buildings. With everyone pitching in and the aid of some hired help, the four float buildings were towed to Refuge Cove, where they were winched ashore. These buildings would soon become the foundation of Ivan's Refuge Cove operations.

The saw-filing shed with the glass roof was remade into the Clarkes' workshop and another building was used as a small cabin. Of the two floating bunkhouses, one was planted on a semi-cleared space between two giant spruce trees and would later become their one-room schoolhouse, and the other would later become a restaurant. Hugh recollected that the two women who rented the restaurant from Ivan had run the Lennard Island lighthouse as well. (The 1948 British Columbia and Yukon Directory lists Florence Nowlan and Fay Sweeny, and it could have possibly been them.) After the restaurant closed down, Ivan rented out the building for people looking for a place to live. He also bought and rented out another building that he winched ashore in front of the old restaurant. Every bit of extra income helped.

Ivan and all of his assistants had everything ready for the first day of school in September 1946. However, an October 27 *Daily Colonist* article out

The Sydney Inlet School opened in 1946 following the arrival of its first teacher, Ivy Myrtle Youell. Ivy lived with her husband, William, in the teacherage (building with porch at right), formerly Annie Emma's cottage. The school is visible just behind the teacherage, with a flagpole to the right. Raymond is at centre.

of Port Alberni, reported that "a teacher had been appointed to the post, but was unable to assume the duties on account of sickness" and the school was expected to open before Christmas. The newspaper also noted that in Refuge Cove, there were only two families that consisted of eleven children. There might have been eleven children, but they were not all of school age. Patsy was only four that September when her name was added to the school enrollment list, as there were not enough school-age pupils to actually open the school. This fudging of the enrollment list was often done when there were not enough school-age children to keep rural schools open. Starting at about age eight or nine, it was up to Hugh to run the school boat up the cove and pick up any students wanting to go to school that day.

The first teacher at the new Sydney Inlet School was Ivy Myrtle (McMahan) Youell, who had been born in Onida, South Dakota. She was about fifty years old and had been married for just two years when she started teaching at Refuge Cove. Her husband, William, was a retired chartered accountant, but he eventually started keeping the books for Ivan's business. They lived in the teacherage, which was formerly Annie Emma's cottage. Mrs. Youell taught up to Grade 8. Higher grades were taught by correspondence, or, as in Nada's case, the student went down to Victoria to live and attended Victoria High School.

Sydney Inlet School was considered to be in an "Unattached District," like Port Renfrew and Bamfield. Like other remote and isolated schools, it had its own special needs and educational requirements.

Since there were not enough local residents to form a school board, Ivan became the solitary official school trustee without being elected. As the only trustee, Ivan had many challenges and demands to work through to improve student achievement. The biggest hurdle, shared with Mrs. Youell, would have been getting the supplies necessary to keep the school running. The government would have provided a budget to pay Mrs. Youell and run the school, but it would have left very little for art supplies, library books and other necessities. Ivan would have had to send in financial and progress reports to the government as often as required.

Ivan was lucky to have hired Ivy Youell. Finding teachers for the remote and isolated schools was difficult, with the result that in some cases poorly qualified teachers had to be hired. Great credit should be given to Ivy for all the years that she spent at Sydney Inlet School. She had more than likely been offered a higher salary in more comfortable surroundings, yet she stayed. This type of devotion is something that money cannot buy.

Claude L. Campbell, the school inspector from Port Alberni, came in once a year by boat from Tofino to do his annual inspection of the school facility and operations. He would check the attendance and student records while sitting quietly, also checking through other paperwork. The children were on their best behaviour, as Mrs. Youell would continue on with her reading, writing and arithmetic lessons with each grade. He would also fill out a yearly teacher report on Mrs. Youell.

The children who attended the school may have fallen short of the refinements and frills that children of the city might enjoy, but they were just as well educated. Students at the Sydney Inlet School also had access to things that children in the city could only dream of: the ocean just a short stroll away from their classroom, wildlife visible from the windows, boats and other vessels to explore nearby, and the hot springs just a thirty minute walk away.

Out at the hot springs was the students' favourite place to hold their annual end of the school year picnic. There was also a small cleared area on the east side of the school by the flagpole where the children could play during the school day. It was about the size of a living room and Ivan had filled in and levelled it. Major George Nicholson wrote, "Lush vegetation is encouraged by the persistent humidity, along with the mild temperatures of the area. In just a few years, other than the roof, the school itself was almost hidden from view by the salal, salmonberries, ferns and other forms of vegetation that grow so profusely all along the coast."

A newspaper article many years ago said that the children were allowed to bring their dogs into the school during classes so that they would not be carried away by bears or a cougar, like Ivan's collie had been on his very first night at the cove. But Hugh said that never happened. Hugh's younger brother Art said that the bears, wolves and cougars never bothered the children because, as he figured, they knew the children were just as wild, if not wilder than they were. Bears did roam the countryside and were seen nearby eating berries, and deer were often seen down by the water.

As Ivan's operation grew, a small Nuu-chah-nulth village also grew across the cove from the store, and at the north end of the cove. A few of those Nuu-chah-nulth children attended the school, but during the fishing season the children moved with their parents when they went to work in the canneries

The rooftops of the Nuu-chah-nulth village are visible on the far side of the cove, at right, in this photograph taken from the roof of the schoolhouse. Several Nuu-chah-nulth children attended the Sydney Inlet School on a seasonal basis. Major George Nicholson Collection/Ken Gibson Collection

and reduction plants at places like Ceepeecee, which was farther up the coast. In the beginning, during most of the year, it was just the Clarke children, along with four Rae-Arthur children, grandchildren of "Cougar Annie," who lived at Boat Basin.

Cougar Annie

Ada Annie Jordan, better known as Cougar Annie, was originally from Sacramento, California. She moved to Boat Basin at the head of Hesquiat Harbour in 1915, owning Clayoquot District Lot 1599, consisting of 117 acres (47.5 hectares). She was known to be feisty and earned her nickname from being a crack shot and claiming to have taken care of at least sixty marauding cougars with her rifle.

She would end up living at Boat Basin for 70 years where she created an extraordinary garden from nothing, one which spanned over 7 acres (3 hectares) of forest. She kept the post office busy with her mail-order nursery/

garden business, shipping seeds, bulbs and plants of all kinds across Canada. Annie outlived four husbands and had eleven children, three of whom died as infants.

After the *Maquinna* was retired, in September 1952, steamer service was never quite the same on the west coast. Annie started to use Ivan to order and purchase some of the supplies for her family, store, nursery and animals. Hugh mentioned that she always seemed to disappear whenever the Clarke boys went up to Boat Basin to collect payment. Annie did not like to part with what little hard-earned money she had.

When she did business with Ivan, in many instances she made payment on her account with her plants and her infamous eggs. Infamous, because Annie was the only one who knew exactly how many days, weeks or months old the eggs really were. Her descendants are still friends with the Clarke family to this day.

Ivan's Lots

While Ivan had been living at the cove, land inspectors from the provincial government Lands Branch would frequently drop by to check out the improvements made and fill out a report on Ivan's progress on their required improvements. It was not until October 12, 1945—shortly before the Refuge Cove school opened—that Ivan returned to the Land Registry office in Victoria, having finally paid the $241 in full that he owed the government for the land, and having done all the improvements required, including having his land properly surveyed. The provincial government gave him the official Crown Land Grant papers for Clayoquot Land District Lot 1372 consisting of 48.2 acres (19.5 hectares). This is the property where he ran his business.

Just over four months later, after paying off the $1,065 in full, and having done all the required improvements, Ivan was given his second Crown Land Grant from the government for Clayoquot Land District Lot 1371, consisting of 213 acres (86 hectares). This lot borders Lot 1372 to the north. He paid for the two lots on the ten-year payment plan, as he called it, which actually took over twelve years.

So by February 20, 1946, Ivan owned all of Openit Peninsula except Ahousaht First Nation Openit No. 27 Reserve, and southern Lots 486 and 697, which is where the hot springs are situated. He eventually acquired a lot

After satisfying the requirements of his Crown Land Grants in 1946, Ivan became the primary landholder of the Openit Peninsula. Improvements continued apace at his general store, including the installation of a new sign. Barker Family Collection/Janine Lampkin Carroll Collection

This 1946 postcard captures the bustle and activity of fishing season at Refuge Cove. Close to two hundred salmon trawlers used the cove as their home base. Major George Nicholson Collection/Ken Gibson Collection

at the northwest end of the cove, and then another couple of lots across the cove from his store after the death of his friend Andreas Thornberg.

Ivan had a new sign professionally painted and fastened to the front of his store. On a 4×8-foot (1.2×2.4-m) piece of white painted plywood it now read:

CLARKE'S
GENERAL STORE
IVAN H. CLARKE SIDNEY INLET

Over the years, a modern store and homes replaced the original structures. Ivan's little store eventually grew into a well-provisioned general store selling everything needed by fishermen, prospectors, timber cruisers, loggers, sailors, tourists on their yachts or private planes, nearby communities and isolated settlers. There was a plumbing and electrical section as well as one for marine and fishing supplies. There were general groceries and canned goods as well as a fruit and vegetable section and a fresh meat–cooler. One could even buy a gun and the ammunition for it. Ivan even updated his "Hot Springs Trail" sign, which he located near the entrance to the store.

Ivan owned many Nuu-chah-nulth masks and carvings. One large carving that he had commissioned of a killer whale was kept outside beside the store, but it eventually rotted away after many years. While unloading supplies one day, Ivan was quite taken aback when a deckhand on the *Maquinna* said he had a body onboard assigned for him. He was much relieved when he found out it was an old free-standing carving he had been waiting for. He had first seen it in Walter T. Dawley's cluttered old workshop in the back of his Clayoquot Hotel on Stubbs Island near Tofino, and subsequently purchased it from Betty Farmer, who had bought the hotel from Walter. For many years, it stood beside Ivan's store. (This carving is still owned by the family.)

Ivan sold Indigenous hand-carved paddles and masks, handmade cedar baskets and other crafts, all at cost to the tourists. He never made money on those sales, just as his son Hugh does not these days. Clarke's General Store and the rest of his Hot Springs Cove operation grew into one of the largest on the west coast of Vancouver Island. In the stories that relatives tell about him today, descriptions of the magnitude of this operation and the amount of land he owned are constantly exaggerated.

By the mid-1940s, Ivan's store carried everything from produce and canned goods to fishing and electrical supplies. On a visit in 1947, legendary Vancouver Island historian Major George Nicholson, right, was photographed wearing a new pair of shoes from Ivan's store. Ivan is on the left. Major George Nicholson Collection/Ken Gibson Collection

By early 1940, Ivan and his brother Ralph had built a cabin about 100 yards (90 m) up the cove from the store for Ralph, his wife, Phyllis, and their new baby daughter, Sheelagh, to come home to from the hospital in Victoria. Eventually the cabin was sold or leased to the Catholic Church to hold services, even though the Clarke family was not Catholic. Ivan later regained ownership of the log building when the Church decided to build a new church of its own at the north end of the cove.

Ralph, and later his family, would live at Refuge Cove from the mid-1930s until 1946. Over the years he was noted to be a labourer, an accountant and the assistant postmaster. In 1947, Ralph and his small family moved to Ucluelet where he worked as a store clerk and then as a storekeeper. For many years they lived in a house on Wickininnish Beach within sight of the original Wickininnish Inn.

Pastimes at the Cove

Ivan's mother, Annie Emma, would have kept herself busy in the evenings with her sewing, crocheting, knitting and fine needlework. Over the years, she won a number of top ribbons and awards at the annual Provincial Fair, and in all the years she was at the cove she continued to have entries in the annual provincial agricultural exhibition. While she was growing up in a Loyalist family in rural New Brunswick, spinning and weaving her own wool would have been a fact of life, taught to her by her mother and grandmother, but her creativity was not limited to using wool, as a short article that ran in the *Daily Colonist* on Sunday, September 7, 1941, made clear.

Fair Exhibitor For Many Years

An interesting exhibitor at the Fall fair is Mrs. W. H. Clarke, who had annual entries in the fair for the past fifty-seven years. Her first entry was a hair wreath, she recalls, made of real hair, and the second year she entered her baby in the baby show and took first prize. This year Mrs. Clarke who is well over eighty, has entries in the embroidery section, to be seen in the women's building.

That winning baby would have been her daughter, Laura May Clarke, born in January 1884. Annie Emma's mother and grandmother would have taught her how to make hair wreaths. There are hair wreaths made by her descendants that have been donated to museums in British Columbia and Alberta. Right from the start, every year Annie Emma took home prize ribbons and she continued to enter, exhibit and win with her handicrafts for many more years at the local Agricultural Fair. Annie Emma would pass away in 1950, but she passed along her talents to her daughters, as well as to some of her granddaughters, my mother being one of them. In turn, my mother taught my two daughters how to crochet and knit.

At the cove, there were few holidays and no shortage of work, but it was not all work and no play for the Clarke children. As a small child, Ray had a bike, which he could ride on his grandmother's small porch and in her kitchen. In a July 3, 1935, letter to her granddaughter Beverley, Annie Emma mentions that a family with five small children was moving to the cove and that Ray would then have some new playmates.

Using their imaginations, the Clarke children spent many hours playing outdoors and having fun by themselves and with the local Nuu-chah-nulth children, as well as any children that might show up along with their parents during the fishing season. In the wintertime, the Clarke and Rae-Arthur children were the only children living there. Much to their mother's displeasure, Hugh remembered, sometimes one or two of the children would climb an alder tree while another cut it down. Then they hung on as the tree fell to the ground and bounced a couple of times before they jumped and rolled away. Art spoke of the same game in a later interview.

Ivan owned a 30-30 rifle that he mainly used for target practice but also for shooting deer and any nuisance bears or cougars, as well as taking a shot at any eagle, hawk or owl that preyed on his chickens. He taught all of his sons how to properly handle a rifle and shoot accurately and safely. Fred Thornberg Jr., a local fisherman and trapper born in Ahousat, taught the Clarke boys to trap. Hugh remembers being taught to trap at the age of ten on the family property. Starting in late fall, they set traps on their land and caught mink, otter and marten. A few days later, armed with a 20-20, they would go out to check their trapline, and empty and reset the traps, using mostly fish for bait.

For all of the animals that they trapped, Fred also showed the boys how to skin, stretch and dry the pelts by themselves on special shaped boards; they then sold the pelts to their father, who was the local fur buyer. Some pelts fetched up to $25 at that time. One day, they were surprised to find one of their traps missing. It took a day or two to locate it and they were even more surprised to find that they had trapped a cougar in it, quite by accident. The animal had managed to break the trap free and carry it a distance away, where it had died. When they found it, Hugh said it was being held in the trap by only one toenail.

In the beginning, when Ivan had purchased from his sons and the Thornbergs enough raw furs to make shipping them worthwhile, he more than likely sent them down to Victoria on the *Maquinna*. A. E. Foster, the president of Foster's Fur Store Ltd. in Victoria, exclusive furriers since 1895, regularly ran ads in the *Daily Colonist* exclaiming: "FUR TRAPPERS! Send us your raw furs by express or postage, collect. We pay highest cash prices."

Eventually, there was a two-room clubhouse built out of recycled lumber, up on the hill beside the trail to the hot springs. There was a workshop and pool table at one end, a card table and a radio in the middle, and at the other end a record player and a Ping-Pong table. While growing up, the children spent a lot of time around the family radio listening to and enjoying their favourite music and programs. Hot Springs Cove was a good place to raise a family: the kids couldn't get into much trouble living out in the bush.

In about the mid-1950s their local Indigenous friends helped the Clarke children clear brush and trees and level the land so they could have their own baseball diamond next to the clubhouse. Hugh said it was not as big as they

Before tourism became the leading industry in Refuge Cove, its residents relied upon Victoria and Vancouver as ready markets for local goods, including furs. In this January 1940 advertisement in the Victoria Daily Colonist, *Foster's Fur Store boasted of "pay[ing] the highest prices for raw furs." This was good news for Ivan's sons, all of whom had learned to trap.* Victoria Daily Colonist

would have liked, but it worked. Unfortunately, William (better known as Billy) was seriously injured during this time, when a cable they were using to winch a stump out of the ground slipped off the top of the stump, let go, whipped back and hit him in the head, just missing Hugh, who was standing right beside him. Billy was rushed out to the Tofino hospital by boat.

Unbeknownst to their father and mother, when the boys were older they had a five-gallon (twenty-two-litre) crock of homebrew hidden in the ceiling of the clubhouse. They used to invite the guys from the visiting American yachts to the clubhouse to listen to music and play pool or Ping-Pong, and then surprise them by offering them a drink of their homebrew. They always had them sign their names in the clubhouse guestbook, which many return guests had forgotten they had signed before, so the brew must have been pretty potent.

CHAPTER 6

Wartime:
Shelling, Boat Seizures, Death

World War II would not leave Refuge Cove unscathed. The first enemy attack on Canadian soil in more than seven decades took place in the area in 1942, and just the year before, the government had started seizing Japanese Canadian fishing boats, many of them along the west coast of Vancouver Island.

In one of the earliest local war-connected tragedies, Ivan's brother Ralph lost his only son, Telegraphist (RCN) Ralph L. Clarke Jr., in the sinking of the Canadian destroyer HMCS *Margaree* on October 22, 1940. Only two and a half months beforehand, Ralph Jr. was married in England to a Miss Ethel Cox. He had earlier received serious injuries in the sinking of the HMCS *Fraser* when the ship had turned the wrong way in the middle of the night and was cut in half by the British cruiser HMCS *Calcutta*. After a long recuperation, he was discharged from the hospital and joined the *Margaree*, the *Fraser*'s replacement ship. Unfortunately, on the return trip to Canada, while escorting convoy OL-8, the *Margaree* was sunk in the North Atlantic after a collision with the freighter *Port Fair*, which cut the ship in half.

As with all war-related deaths of Victorians, Ralph's death made the front page of the city's newspapers.

Refuge Cove was not immune to wartime tragedy. In October 1940, Ivan's nephew Ralph L. Clarke Jr. was killed while serving on the HMCS Margaree, a Canadian destroyer. Just months earlier, Ralph had married Ethel Martha Cox in England. Sheelagh (Clarke) Varga Family Collection

Ralph Jr.'s passing was followed a couple of years later by a bittersweet event. In 1942, with the war still raging, his young widow travelled from England to Refuge Cove to keep a promise. As a new bride, Ethel (Cox) Clarke had vowed to her husband that should he die during the war, she would visit his family at Refuge Cove. So, as a twenty-three-year-old war widow, with hostilities continuing in the Atlantic, Ethel made her way, by herself, from Enfield, Middlesex, England to Refuge Cove to visit the Clarkes. She eventually settled down in Victoria, where she remarried and had a family. Ethel (Cox) Coulter passed away in Victoria in 2013.

Shameful Dispossession

A year after Ralph Jr.'s death, the war left a particularly nasty imprint on the west coast of Vancouver Island and the rest of British Columbia.

Two years after entering World War II, Canada declared war on Japan on December 7, 1941. In an article titled, "The Japanese Threat: Impounded on the West Coast: Navy, Part 47," Marc Milner describes how, two days later, the 205-foot corvette HMCS *Quesnel* seized all the Japanese Canadian fishing vessels along the west coast of Vancouver Island. The size of the government vessels and the weapons aboard would have been intimidating, but Japanese Canadian fishermen co-operated with the seizure in the belief that they would get their boats back. This belief, it turned out, was completely false. "The seizure of Japanese Canadian fishing boats, therefore, became the first act in Canada's shameful dispossession and forced removal of Japanese Canadians from the coast of BC."

Most of the Japanese Canadian boat owners took their own boats down to Annieville on the Fraser River, where approximately twelve hundred of them were eventually impounded. The long line of boats were escorted down the west coast of the island under guard of the Fishermen's Reserve vessel, the 130-foot *Givenchy*, with a soldier placed aboard each fishboat.

On December 16, all Japanese Canadians were banned outright from operating any sort of boat in British Columbia waters "without expressed permission." Fishermen who Ivan had known for years had their boats seized and eventually the fishermen and their families were relocated and sent to internment camps in the interior of British Columbia. Members of the Clarke family stayed in touch with their displaced Japanese Canadian friends for many years after.

"The treatment of Japanese Canadians after Dec. 7, 1941 remains one of the most discreditable events in Canadian history," Milner concludes.

A couple of months after the start of the boat seizures, the Sunday, February 15, 1942, edition of the *Daily Colonist* carried a full-page ad headed with the banner "Let These Men Help You Buy Canada's Victory Loans." In the middle of the page was a mock certificate for a Victory Loan that said "Certificate of Honour, The Government of the Dominion of Canada, gratefully acknowledge that A Loyal Citizen has aided Canada's War Effort, by investing in the Second Victory Loan 1942." The names of the people you could purchase the Victory Loans from in Unit "H" Alberni District for the west coast of Vancouver Island included Ivan Clarke at Refuge Cove.

Lighthouse Attacked

On June 20, 1942, just over six months after the Japanese attack on Pearl Harbor, a Japanese submarine fired up to thirty shells at Estevan Point Lighthouse, not far to the northwest of Refuge Cove. It was the first enemy attack on Canadian soil since the Fenian Raids in 1866 and 1871. During those years the Irish Republican organization Fenian Brotherhood, based in the United States, made raids on British army forts, customs posts and other important targets in Canada hoping to put pressure on Britain to withdraw from Ireland.

The shelling of the lighthouse occurred a few days after the submarine had torpedoed and sunk the coastal freighter the ss *Coast Trader* at the mouth of Juan de Fuca Strait. Along with a few others, these two events sowed panic all along the BC and US Pacific northwest coast, bringing home the danger and reality of the war in the Pacific.

The *Daily Colonist* ran the following article out of Zeballos on June 23.

More Than One Ship in Estevan Point Shelling

Zeballos—Ben Thomas, an Indian fisherman, told tonight how exploding shells from enemy craft attacking the radio station at Estevan Point caused Indians to flee their homes on a nearby reservation in night attire and seek safety in their boats in Hesquiat Harbor six miles away.

The Indian, Ben Thomas reached here from Estevan Point, forty-five miles northward up the west coast of Vancouver Island, with the first eyewitness account of the half hour shelling, which Defence

Minister Ralston said at Ottawa today was carried out by possibly two enemy craft.

"Shells whizzed over my home on the Indian reservation on the point," Thomas said. "There were about nineteen shots, but none did any damage. I was plenty scared and so were my neighbors and we raced for our boats. Some of the Indians were just going to bed when the firing started and fled to the safety in their boats only partially dressed."

CLOSE TO LIGHT

Thomas said that only one shell landed close to the lighthouse, which is beside the radio station on Estevan Point.

"The shells smashed a lot of rock beyond the reserve. It was poor shooting" he added.

The Indian fisherman said the lightkeeper at Estevan Point shut off his light when the attack began.

The Indians who took to their boats sought refuge in a bay known as Boat Basin, which actually forms the Harbor of Hesquiat, nearest settlement to Estevan Point.

The Saturday night attack was the first direct assault of the war on Canadian soil, but failed to cause any damage. The shells from the attacker's guns landed short or beyond the radio station and lighthouse. Only damage was to a few windows in the radio station, smashed by concussion.

In the *Daily Colonist* on June 24, 1942, on page eight, the following article appeared, datelined Port Alberni, June 23.

Climbs Ladder to Extinguish Light
Action of Estevan Lightkeeper and Radio Operator
Highly Courageous During Japanese Attack

–Women Spent Night in Woods–

While residents of the West Coast are continuing to discuss the shelling of Estevan Point, the residents of that small Government settlement are describing the courageous act of the lightkeeper, Robert Mitchell Lally, who while shells screamed around him climbed the fifty-foot ladder to extinguish the powerful light which was throwing its beam many miles to sea.

At the regulation time after sundown, he climbed to the top of the tower to remove the canvas cover and set his light going. This is one of the most powerful lights on the coast and is used by ships far out at sea to pick up their bearings and plot their course when approaching the land. Little did he think he was probably setting a beacon for an enemy war craft which might have meant the destruction of residents of the settlement.

Other employees with their wives and families were preparing for the night. Brian Harrison, radio operator, and Mrs. Harrison, were having tea with Edward King Redford, radio operator, and Mrs. Redford. Mrs. Harrison was a little worried over the Pacific war on account of her seven-months'-old baby. At about 10:30 the silence was shattered by the scream and explosion of a shell. The first thought of everyone was that one of the engines had exploded and the employees rushed to the doors of their homes. Then a second and a third scream and explosion of shells.

BUILDING TREMBLED

The flashes at sea in the darkness soon told them that the enemy were bombarding the settlement. The first shells landed near the shore at the foot of the lighthouse and the solid concrete building trembled. Another shell and the concussion broke several windows. It was then that Lally realized that the light was a beacon for the guns, and with shells screaming and bursting about the lighthouse he climbed around and around the spiral staircase to the top where he extinguished the light, just as the enemy, realizing they were shooting low, raised their elevation and the shells passed alongside the light and exploded in the woods behind.

In the meantime, Redford and an assistant were in the radio room, sending out to authorities news of the attack. Every moment they expected the building would be blown to pieces. But it was not until the light had been put out and news of the attack had been forwarded did the men think of themselves.

Gathering the women together, without blankets and wearing only what they had on at the time of the firing, they were hurried in the darkness to the woods behind the station. It seemed then as if the Japanese knew they had taken shelter in the woods, for the elevation was raised from shooting at the foot of the lighthouse into the woods. But the elevation had been raised too high, and the shells went screaming overhead while the women and children lay hidden among the trees.

COMFORTED BABY

The first thought of Mrs. Brian Harrison was for her seven-month-old baby, and as the children and women lay hidden in the timber until daylight she comforted it as best she could. At daylight everyone returned to the lighthouse and radio building, not knowing whether the enemy had made a landing or not, but all satisfied that the men had stuck to their jobs and done their duty well. Later in the morning airplanes and a fishery patrol boat arrived at the scene.

Mrs. Redford and Mrs. Harrison with her seven-month-old child arrived in Port Alberni yesterday, but refused to be interviewed, still feeling the effects of their ordeal.

Of great interest in town during the day was the nosecap of a four-inch shell which had been picked up on the rocks. This was painted very black with white Japanese writing on it.

Residents of Estevan state that during the day a surface craft was seen loitering off-shore but they presumed it was a friendly ship and did not take any particular notice of it. A road crew from Port Alberni is at Estevan fixing a road to Hesquiat.

The attack on the lighthouse was followed by Japanese balloon bombs, which happened during 1944–45, also known as fire balloon attacks. They consisted of a hydrogen balloon, carrying anywhere from a 26-pound (12-kg) incendiary bomb up to a 33-pound (15-kg) antipersonnel bomb, along with four 11-pound (5-kg) incendiary devices. They were designed as an inexpensive weapon, intended to make use of the jet stream over the Pacific Ocean and drop their bombs on whatever they happen to hit in North America

Hugh and Nada were living with their Stephen grandparents and going to school in Victoria at the time of the Estevan shelling, but years later Ivan told Hugh that he had been ready to chop the fuel lines and set the water on fire if the enemy entered the cove. They did not have any issues with the enemy fire balloons at the cove, but during those years, even if they had been balloon bombed, it would have been kept quiet because the government did not want the news to get back to Japan that their balloons were making it all the way across the ocean.

Civilians and Upgrades

One of the best-kept secrets of World War II was the Vancouver Island civilians who served in the Royal Canadian Navy. At the beginning of October 1945, Ivan received a letter of appreciation from Hon. Douglas Abbott, minister of defence. Through his position as a west coast postmaster, along with his maritime background, Ivan had been appointed by the Royal Canadian Navy to be a "naval reporting officer." He was trained in naval coding and his job was to supply the Royal Canadian Navy with full information on coastwise shipping, reporting all ships sighted and all arrivals and departures. He served with little or no remuneration. His reporting officer in Victoria was Gerald A. Yardley, collector of customs.

In December 1945, the Dominion government was putting together estimates for capital projects. Some of this money was to go into harbour improvements. It was estimated it would cost $1000 to put the float at Refuge Cove in good repair again. Three years later as part of the address by the liberal organizer for British Columbia to the Alberni District Liberal Association, it was brought up that docks, sheds, light and a fog horn were needed at Refuge Cove, as aids to boats seeking shelter there, and as a means of better supplying Estevan Point.

On August 28, 1945, the British Columbia Provincial Executive Council sent a letter to the lieutenant-governor appointing Ivan as a provincial election commissioner for Sydney Inlet in the Alberni Electoral District for the upcoming election, without pay. On April 21, 1953, the council sent another letter, this time appointing Ivan as a deputy registrar of voters for Hot Springs

Cove in the Alberni Electoral District for the upcoming election. This letter was signed by W. A. C. Bennett, then premier of British Columbia. Ivan held similar positions for all the other provincial elections and the same position for all the Dominion government elections while he was at the cove.

In 1946, Mabel's younger brother, Patrick Stephen, moved up to the cove and worked as a fish buyer. He lived there until about 1950. Until the early 1940s, other than the Clarkes, there had been only one non-Indigenous man living full time at the cove with his family: George Rae-Arthur, a BC Telephone lineman.

In an indication of his life at the cove around this time, Ivan's eldest son, Ray, wrote a letter to his mother in May 1947 thanking her for her letter and the chocolates that she had sent up to him. He told her how he spent his seventeenth birthday, several days earlier, trout fishing. It was the first time, he said, that he had enjoyed himself since moving up to Refuge Cove. It had rained all the day before, but the sun was shining on the day he wrote his letter. There were lots of fishboats moored in the cove but no fish being caught, so he hadn't had much to do for the previous few days. Missing the time he had been able to spend in the city, he asked if he had missed any good shows or if there was such a thing as a good show. A month earlier in a letter to his mother he mentioned how some boys from the other fish camps were already swimming in the cove, but he said he was waiting for the water to warm up a bit more. The *Colonist* noted that Mabel's mom, Mary Stephen, spent the summers of 1943 and 1947 visiting the Clarke family, but she was probably up there most summers. Most of Ivan's siblings and their spouses also came up to visit over the years.

Light Plant, Other Upgrades

In the early years, there was no electricity in the cove. Any nighttime activity such as cooking, cleaning, reading or playing was done by the light of coal oil lanterns and later by Coleman lanterns. Every day the glass chimneys had to be cleaned, wicks cut and the tanks filled. Both Mabel and Nada enjoyed reading. My mother was also a voracious reader and encouraged my daughters, Olivia and Hannah, to read. The Clarke family as well as any guests, would also play card games such as bridge and crib well into the night by the light of the lanterns.

Refuge Cove was only the second Standard Oil fuel depot on the west coast of Vancouver Island. Fuel was delivered regularly by the BC *Standard.* Major George Nicholson Collection/Ken Gibson Collection

Early on, Ivan had become the agent for Standard Oil Company selling stove oil, diesel, marine fuel, Avgas (aviation gas) and other Standard Oil products to the fishermen, tourists and anyone else who showed up in a boat or float plane. Tofino had the first Standard Oil fuel depot on the west coast of Vancouver Island, followed shortly thereafter when Ivan started the second Standard Oil depot at Refuge Cove.

After working as Standard Oil's agent for many years, on January 24, 1955, Ivan gave the Standard Oil Company of British Columbia a 20-year lease on part of his property, which could be renewed for another ten years. Fuel was delivered regularly by the company's BC *Standard* and, starting in 1959, fuel was delivered by its brand new ship of the same name, the 162-foot BC *Standard*, filling Ivan's 11,000-gallon (50,000-L) diesel and marine fuel tanks, as well as all the other tanks. Avgas was delivered by the barrel.

In the early 1940s, Standard Oil provided the first light plant for the house, store and fuel dock. The light plant was mainly used in the evenings, as the windows supplied enough light in the store and house during the daytime. Ivan took care of running and maintaining the light plant until the boys got older and took over the job, starting with Ray. The fuel tank was filled at dusk

*When this bunkhouse ran aground in the late 1940s, Ivan used materials from it to build
a new home for his family.* W.J. Bowerman Collection, care of Ian Haynes

and the light plant would run until it ran out of gas, usually around midnight.
They would add a bottle of gas on top of the tank just to make it run a bit
longer.

In the later 1940s, Canadian Fishing Company installed a new much-
larger light plant, which supplied enough power for their home, the store,
school, teacherage, restaurant, fish camp, fuel dock and all the other buildings. Hugh built a metal-clad building down near the water on the south
side of the wharf for the new power plant, and it was also used as a tool shed.
The building still exists. During the war years the government had a wind-
powered battery installation at the cove.

Also in the later 1940s, a large scow with bunkhouses fastened on its
deck broke free from the tug that was towing it and ran aground a mile
or so south of Estevan Point, about 12 miles (19 km) away from Refuge
Cove. This type of floating bunkhouse would typically have been used in
coastal construction camps, sawmills, logging camps or canneries. Ivan
acquired the rights to the scow and bunkhouses from Mr. E. Savey from
Gold River, who owned the salvage rights.

Ivan hired a few local friends to tear the bunkhouses apart and haul
all the material back to his property at Refuge Cove, to use to upgrade his
own buildings. This included eventually building a new four-bedroom

home attached to the north side of the store for his family. There were four new wood stoves in the bunkhouses, which Ivan sold to local logging camps. About a year later, he sold the barge to a man in Port Alberni who successfully refloated and repaired it.

In other news from that time, in 1947 it was reported that there was a relatively small herring spawn in Refuge Cove—usually an important spawning ground. Only about 9,500 tons were taken from the Clayoquot Sound area during that fishing season. Normally the herring would spawn heavily up and down the cove, even under Ivan's dock.

In a July 8, 1947, *Daily Colonist* article about increased interest in the towns of Alberni and Port Alberni as a shipping centre, it was noted by the Gibson Transportation Company that since their ship, the former submarine chaser, 108-foot 3-inch *Machigonne*, had gone into service "shipments of milk to the West Coast exceeded 400 gallons [1,816 L] per month. At Refuge Cove shipments of ice cream are being received because of the fast two-way service." Gibson's also briefly used the *Machigonne* in 1947 to transport longshoremen, workers and freight from Port Alberni to its sawmill in Tahsis, at the head of Tahsis Inlet farther up the west coast of Vancouver Island.

New Name, New Faces: *Hot Springs Cove Draws Marine Tourists*

There was some confusion in getting the mail to the cove, and to help clarify exactly where his post office was, Ivan wanted to change the name from Sydney Inlet Post Office to Refuge Cove Post Office. He applied for the name change, but was denied because there was already a Refuge Cove Post Office on the south end of East Redonda Island, at the entrance to Homfray Channel, near Powell River, so he reapplied using the name Hot Springs Cove Post Office.

On May 22, 1948, Postmaster Ivan Clarke was sent a package containing a letter from Frederick H. Middlemiss, the Vancouver District Post Office inspector, telling him that advice had been received from the postal department that on Saturday, October 23, 1948, the Sydney Inlet Post Office would officially change its name to Hot Springs Cove Post Office. The letter also advised him that the new date-stamping equipment would be received in the near future and would be forwarded to him as soon as it came in. Also enclosed was a poster with notice of information about the name change, which Ivan was asked to post in a prominent location readily visible for all his patrons to read.

That same year Hot Springs Cove was listed for the first time in the BC and Yukon Directory. The entry made mention of a post office at Refuge Cove, 25 miles (40km) north of Clayoquot, on the west coast of Vancouver Island. It also indicated a population of 63 people. It was not until the 1953 directory that "Formerly Refuge Cove" was also noted.

By royal proclamation, "Harbour of Hot Springs Cove" was declared to be a public harbour on January 18, 1949. But it wasn't until a decade later—in 1959—that the official name change was publicly confirmed and the new name, Hot Springs Cove, appeared on the newly printed marine chart.

1950s Tourists

In the early 1950s tourists started to arrive at Hot Springs Cove on their yachts and cabin cruisers, and there were some who took advantage of the float planes that had started to fly tourists into the area. At the beginning of the decade, the boating industry rapidly started growing, thanks to the thousands of middle-class buyers who could now afford and enjoy the pleasures of cruising with their families. In July 30, 1950, the *Daily Colonist* carried an article about three Seattle cabin cruiser owners, one an old friend of Ivan's, who decided to come up the west coast of Vancouver Island instead of taking the sheltered east coast that they would normally use on their yearly trip north to Alaska, as did most owners of pleasure craft wanting to explore the waters of BC.

They stopped especially to visit with Ivan at Hot Springs Cove. This was great for Ivan. Word was slowly getting out about his operation at Hot Springs Cove and now more tourists on their yachts and cruisers from the west coast of British Columbia, Washington, Oregon and California would hopefully start to come up the outside of the island and make stops to see him and visit the hot springs.

The *Colonist* article read as follows.

Port Alberni, July 29—The occasional yacht or cruiser drops into Port Alberni, but on Thursday, three of the finest cruisers from the Queen City Yacht Club of Seattle visited this port.

These cruisers had made a leisurely trip from Seattle and their owners and families, who have been cruising and fishing Barkley

Sound for the past few days, report a pleasant trip. All have taken part in international and national cruises and have often made the trip to Alaska by inside waters. They thought they would try on [*sic*] outside trip this year.

They have met some heavy weather in places on the way up, but all the boats behaved well and there was no delay.

NAVAL ARCHITECT

Two of the cruisers were designed by Ed Monk, naval architect, who has designed several boats for fishermen and others in this vicinity. The new boat of Reese Riley, harbour commissioner, was designed by him, and the Port Alberni shipyards are now building a Monk-designed boat for Fred Osborne.

The visiting cruisers are Ersal Davis' [fifty-four foot] "Chilton," Ed Monk's [thirty-nine foot] "Alerion" and Dick Taylor's [thirty-four foot] "Como Reto."

Mr. Taylor used to fish the West Coast and at one time packed fish from Barkley Sound with his father. He had taken part in nearly every international and national race in these waters since 1936 and holds a third prize and a second in cruiser events.

Mr. Taylor has another distinction. He holds the clam-eating championship of the world, won by polishing off 274 clams in ten minutes. At the Seattle Boat Show last year, against 12 contenders from the Atlantic to the Pacific, he beat his nearest competitor by 60 clams. Mr. Taylor says they were beach-run clams from the butter clam to the ordinary rough corrugated shell.

ENJOYS FJORDS

Mr. Taylor is also the fisherman of the crowd, but all are enjoying themselves in the long fiords of the West Coast. They will proceed from here to Clayoquot Sound and Tofino Inlet, will spend a few days with Ivan Clarke at Hot Springs Cove and then travel leisurely back to Seattle.

The arrival of these cruisers here and the interest of the owners in the West Coast may be the means of making the West Coast trip a must for many Washington and California yachtsmen.

Mr. Taylor has already had six television shows presented throughout the United States of his travels to Alaska by the inside passage. He will endeavor to publicize the west coast in the same way.

As the cove offers one of the safest anchorages between Victoria and Cape Scott on the northern tip of Vancouver Island, almost all small craft that travelled up or down the west coast of Vancouver Island dropped in to see Ivan and the hot springs. As harbour master, Ivan was keeping track of all the boats that came and went. By 1954, he reported that as many as 50 yachts and cruisers had called in over the summer. Word was getting out that the "treacherous waters" of Vancouver Island's west coast were not so dangerous after all. At the right time of year and with the weather in their favour, boaters were discovering attractions like the hot springs and finding them to be easily accessible for every type of boat.

Ivan recorded that of the fifty vessels that called in over the summer, half of them were American, visiting from locations as near as Puget Sound and as far as California. The Canadian boats that called in were mainly from Vancouver and Victoria. Ivan also recorded that by 1958, only one in five pleasure boats and private aircraft were Canadian. More American pleasure craft owners were exploring the west coast of Vancouver Island than Canadians were. Captain Reese Riley, owner of the *Maureen R.*, was the son of Reece Riley Sr., whom Riley's Cove on the northwest tip of Flores Island was named after. It was where Ivan had to go to pick up his supplies and mail when he first moved to Refuge Cove. Captain Riley and his new speedboat-cruiser *Maureen R.* (named after his daughter) were lost off Flores Island late on a stormy afternoon just over three months after the three cruisers' visit, when Riley was bound from Port Alberni to Hot Springs Cove for the night. His body was never found. Although the wreckage was found near Rafael Point on the west coast of Flores Island, the cause of the wreck of the *Maureen R.* remains a mystery to this day.

Coincidently, in 1961, Benson Shipyard Company in Vancouver was contracted to build four 47-foot (14-m) bridge-deck cruisers designed by Edwin Monk, the designer of the *Maureen R.* One was built especially for Harold Elworthy, Ivan's former brother-in-law, which Harold named *Lady Diane*, for his daughter. It was one of the largest cruisers in the area at that time, and the only one of the four that was diesel powered. In more recent years, the now renamed cruiser has become a wooden boat show prize winner.

Life at Hot Springs Cove

Cove life was not without the occasional emergency. On Wednesday, January 18, 1950, Ivan made a phone call for a "Mercy Flight" out of the cove. Pilot Lawrence Mantie flew in a sleek Seabee amphibian plane owed by Port Alberni Air Lines. Seventy-eight-year-old William Youell was suffering great pains from severe abdominal complications, the consequence of a pleurisy attack two weeks earlier. The 135-mile (216-km) air trip to Stewart Avenue Air Base in Esquimalt took about an hour and 50 minutes, with William's wife, Ivy, accompanying him. They arrived to find about a foot of snow. Although it was a smooth trip, it was very cold. The Victoria Ambulance Service then rushed William to the Royal Jubilee Hospital. He told the two ambulance attendants it was so cold that he was going to move back to the prairies.

This flight was front-page news the next day in Victoria. Interestingly, after spending an hour and a half at the hospital he was told he was not sick enough to be admitted. The next day another doctor found him seriously ill enough to be admitted to St. Joseph's Hospital. William survived, and as he had said he would, he did end up moving back to the prairies, where he passed away nine years after making front-page news. Ivy passed away in 1986 in Victoria.

In the early 1950s, just over 60 people lived at Hot Springs Cove, which had become the headquarters for a Vancouver Island west coast fishing fleet. During the eight-month fishing season up to nine fish-buying camps were added to the mix in the cove, along with their own seasonal general stores, which rivalled Ivan's. Ivan ran two fish camps, one a co-op and the other owned by Canadian Fishing Company. He had his share of faithful fishermen and friends that he knew well, who he could rely on to sell their fish to his fish camps and shop at his store. Along the way, the co-op fish camp decided to break off on its own.

There was now a fish camp owned by the Fishermen's Co-op; the others were owned by the McLellans, BC Packers, Pallister (who eventually ended up in Sooke), J. F. Todd & Sons and some other independents. All of these

Hot Springs Cove teemed with fishing boats and fish camps during the eight-month fishing season. Ivan's fish camp was conveniently the first camp a boat would encounter as it returned to the cove. Major George Nicholson Collection/Ken Gibson Collection

fish camps and their stores were on large rafts moored to the shore. Ivan's camp was the first one the fishboats had to pass by when they entered the cove. If, in the very early morning hours, a fishboat could be heard coming in, it was not unusual for one of the Clarke boys to jump out of bed, race down to their fish camp, wave the boat over and scoop the sale from one of the other camps. At that time of the morning the fisherman really didn't care; he just wanted to unload and sell his fish, and get some well-earned sleep.

Every morning, a call would be made to Canadian Fishing Company to let them know how much fish was in their camp. During the off-season, the other fish-buying camps were towed away by their owners. As both Hugh and Art and the rest of the brothers were mechanically adept and had learned to fix everything and anything along the way, Ivan was able to also add marine repairs to his ever-expanding enterprise. Although there was not a machine shop, per se, at Hot Springs Cove, they owned all the tools they needed for marine repairs, which they kept in the tool shed. By 1953, Ivan had torn down his original log cabin and store to make way for further expansion.

Every evening, the fishermen would haul in their catches and sell it to Ivan's fish camp. They'd spend the rest of the evening doing minor repairs, filling up with ice, refuelling and shopping if needed. Then they'd eat dinner and go to bed in their bunks. That was the basic life of a fisherman. According to Art, back then "all the equipment a fisherman needed was a boat, lead line, his fishing gear and a compass." The fishing industry has very much changed since then.

Storm days were called "harbour days," when the boats made their way back and gathered in the cove. In the years before Ivan arrived, if the boats were holed up for too long in the cove the fishermen would be forced onto a diet of clams, which could be found in abundance on any decent beach. The other option was to try and bag a goose or duck if it came into range. Fortunately, even during the Depression when money was very tight they could at least get some credit through Ivan to buy food and gear as needed.

Harbour days could easily last from one day to a week. The cove would be packed with boats of all shapes and sizes. The first trollers in were lucky and would be tied up eight abreast or more on the inside and outside of Ivan's float. It was a good chance for the fishermen to catch up on news from the outside world, repair their boats and equipment, and stock up for their next journey. They would also embark on the short walk to the hot springs to bathe and do their laundry. They had a free, unlimited supply of hot water to boil their laundry in. If they woke up to a nice morning, the cove would quickly become deserted.

The *Princess Maquinna* became one of the regular visitors to the cove. When Ivan first arrived, the ship was on a 10-day schedule, only dropping by if there was cargo to unload. Under the 1948 CPR summer schedule, the ship stopped at the cove every eight days. As Ivan's operation grew, Hugh recalled the days when the *Maquinna* called on Hot Springs Cove about once a week, usually on a Friday. My father, Barry Kaehn, who had met my mother in Victoria, worked as a fireman on the Princess ships during the late 1940s and early '50s and could remember the ship he was on dropping anchor, or sometimes just drifting in Hot Springs Cove while his future father-in-law rowed out in his 20-foot (6.1-m) freight rowboat along with future brothers- and sisters-in-law, to be loaded up with supplies, as the boats bobbed up and down in the surf. This was called a "boat landing."

Because there was not a large enough wharf to accommodate the ship, and the ship was not stopped long enough, *Maquinna*'s passengers could not get out to enjoy the hot springs.

On "boat day" one of Raymond's jobs was to bail the rainwater out of the freight rowboat before the *Maquinna* arrived, as did the other boys—and even Patsy—as they grew older. They would wait for the *Maquinna* to enter the cove and blow her familiar long-short-long-short whistle. Patsy would then go out in the rowboat with the others, as it was her job to jump onto the deck of the ship and run up the inside staircases to the main deck to pick up the pile of newspapers destined for the cove. Sometimes she had to be fast so as not to be left behind, so she would throw the papers down the stair-case and bound down after them, and then do the same to the next flights of

Prior to the construction of a larger wharf in 1952, all goods arriving on the Maquinna *were shuttled into Hot Springs Cove, frequently by Ivan's children, aboard his 20-foot freight boat. Raymond, with oars, delivers cargo to the shore with Hugh's help.*

stairs until she finally had them on the deck just above water level, ready to be loaded into the freight boat.

Everyone looked forward to boat day as it was also mail day. Originally all the mail came in on the *Maquinna*, then by North Arm Transport and later

The new Dominion government wharf and floats (left and centre) allowed supply ships to make deliveries directly to Ivan's store, visible at bottom right. Major George Nicholson Collection/Ken Gibson Collection

by airline. Regular mail as well as parcels bought through Eaton's, Hudson's Bay Company, Simpsons-Sears and Woodward's stores and through other mail-order catalogues would arrive, so the post office would be very busy on boat day.

There were very few ways of spending your hard-earned money in isolated places like Hot Springs Cove, so mail order became a very popular way of spending it, and if you needed a postal money order to pay for your mail order, Ivan's post office had those ready to fill out. It's likely Ivan was also the unofficial banker, cashing paycheques, if need be.

In 1952, the Dominion government put out a tender for new wharves and approaches at the cove. William E. Bond of Tofino was awarded the contract with the final cost coming in at $23,409. Even though Public Works and Government Services Canada had the new wharves and approaches built, it was not until June 4, 1955, that the provincial government Crown granted the Dominion government's Public Works the land the structures were occupying.

Until the new wharf and floats were built, everything was lowered down several feet from the *Maquinna*'s large metal side doors to Ivan's big freight boat. Even though it was usual to sit and row the loaded-up freight boat, some of Ivan's sons found it easier to stand facing forward and push on the oars to take the boat out and guide it back to shore. Hugh eventually installed a small engine in the boat. The freight boat was Ivan's main means of water transportation, other than taking the *Maquinna*, until he purchased a 24-foot (7.3-m) wooden-hulled boat with a bit of a cabin on it.

Maquinna *Stops Sailing*

During the month of August 1952, there were stories floating around about the *Maquinna* going in for boiler inspection on September 24, possibly to run no more, which caused a lot of excitement up and down the coast as well as in Victoria. News of the termination of service brought forward speculation of other companies taking over. One possible replacement for the *Maquinna* was the 172-foot 6-inch *Chilkoot*, built in 1919 and owned by the Waterhouse Shipping concern, which was already doing a run near the top end of the island, and at first it did replace the *Maquinna* for a few round trips.

On September 3, 1952, a *Daily Colonist* front-page headline announced, "Boiler Finished, Old Maquinna Limps into Port." The *Maquinna*'s boilers could no longer raise the steam needed, reducing its speed from 14 knots to 9 knots. Combined with there being less cargo and fewer passengers than in its heyday years, this resulted in the end of the ship's sailing days.

According to the article, Captain Carthew, the *Maquinna*'s last master, assembled his passengers in the ship's salon and informed them that the ship had made its last trip and would sail no more. The passengers would be permitted to stay on the ship that night, as many had already retired for the night, and they would also be provided breakfast in the morning. After that they were on their own to find their way up the coast as best they could.

In 1953, after the *Princess Maquinna*'s days of serving the west coast ended, her hull was stripped down in North Vancouver at Clarence Wallace's Burrard Dry Dock shipyard. The ship was converted into a non-powered barge for Straits Towing and renamed the *Bulk Carrier Taku*, used for carrying ore concentrates for Consolidated Mining and Smelting Company from

After four decades of service along the west coast of Vancouver Island, the Princess Maquinna *returned to port for the last time on September 2, 1952. Ivan attended the initial dismantling of the* Maquinna, *where he purchased its keys as a souvenir.*

Tulsequah, BC, north to Juneau, Alaska. In 1963 the barge was scrapped by General Shipbreaking Company of Vancouver.

Ivan had a fondness for the *Maquinna*, recalling his initial trip north on the ship in 1933 to start his store, his marriage onboard in 1935, bringing his newborn babies home, the many times he travelled up and down the west coast on the ship; as well as all the years of service it gave to him at Hot Springs Cove. So he paid his respects by attending the initial dismantling of the *Maquinna*. There he purchased as a souvenir all of the ship's keys, including the stateroom keys, which are still in the possession of the Clarke family today. His ex-brother-in-law, Harold Elworthy, was able to obtain the flagpole off the *Maquinna* to use in the Island Tug & Barge Marine Garden on Harbour Road in Victoria, and the boat's rich-toned bell was in the perpetual care of the Missions to Seamen in Vancouver and was used for the call to worship in their chapel. The *Maquinna*'s compass and binnacle were given to the Ucluelet Sea Cadets.

After the Maquinna

When the *Maquinna* was retired, the Canadian Pacific Railway Company's 149-foot 1-inch *Princess of Alberni*, built in 1945, began to stop at the cove every Sunday on its northbound voyage only. Ivan and George Nicholson both championed for better transportation service to the west coast of Vancouver Island. For as many years as Ivan, Nicholson had been running a similar operation to his at Zeballos, holding many of the same jobs and government-related positions as Ivan did. Neither of them was going to be happy until a better steamer replaced the late *Maquinna*. Both thought the 10,000 residents of the west coast deserved a vessel at least as large as the *Maquinna* had been. If that could not be done, they figured that a smaller vessel could be used in the winter as long as a regular-sized passenger ship was still in service in the summer, considering that the west coast was a popular tourist destination in the summer.

The cove could also be reached by private boat or by Queen Charlotte Airlines until 1955, and after that by BC Airlines, for both of which Ivan was the airline agent. In 1953 Pacific Western Airlines proposed to serve points within 12.5 miles (20kkm) on both sides of a straight line drawn from Port Alberni to Tofino. This would include locations such as Sydney Inlet, Nootka, Zebal-

The Princess of Alberni *replaced the* Maquinna *along the west coast of Vancouver Island, much to the chagrin of Ivan and George Nicholson, who insisted the area deserved a better vessel.* Major George Nicholson Collection/Ken Gibson Collection

los and more. Flight frequency and cost would be based entirely on public demand, with rates levied on a per pound basis.

For most of the year, strong winds are common in the afternoon on this part of Vancouver Island. In late summer, when the winds are calm, the cove would be completely enveloped in an advection fog (created when warm moist air moves horizontally across the surface of the ocean). It wasn't unusual to be socked in by the weather, people having to wait up to two weeks for a flight in or out.

Business was good for Ivan. During the fishing season in the mid-1950s, up to 400 boats would visit the cove to sell their fish and stock up on supplies and fuel. Hugh recounted, "Although the Nuu-chah-nulth community across the cove had a decent beach, they did not have the facilities to dock their boats, so they used to anchor them and row ashore. If it got too stormy, they would move across the cove and moor their boats at Ivan's wharf." There were no roads or sidewalks, only boardwalks and trails, so there were no two- or four-wheel vehicles at the cove.

Over the years the BC Forest Service boat stationed at Tofino, the 48-foot 7-inch *Yellow Cedar* (formerly the *Bonilla Rock*, which had been built in 1914), would stop at the cove at the end of work trips visiting west coast logging camps. The crew would make a point of stopping for an unofficial visit with Ivan and then head out to the hot springs for an evening bath.

According to Patsy, her mother, Mabel, was "the work shoes and brains of the factory, she was the one that kept the place going." Ivan hired one of the Campbell girls from the village, who helped Mabel around the house and with the children. Besides caring for the cats and dogs that the children had as pets, as they grew up they became more involved in the family business. One of Jimmy's daily chores was to feed his chickens and collect their eggs, some of which were sold to Ivan's boating customers. As meat was hard to come by, at the end of their lives the chickens became Sunday dinner for the family.

One of Patsy's first jobs was to go down to the wharf to get ice from the fish-camp barge for the pop machine in the store. This was actually a two-child job so Art or Jimmy also helped carry the washtub of ice back up to the store. There was no charge for anyone wanting ice.

Starting at about ten years of age, Patsy was at the side counter selling gum, chocolate bars, ice cream and magazines. She soon moved up to the main counter. Sometimes the girls would stock shelves until three in the morning and would often go to bed when the boats were heading out to fish for the day. Patsy changed the bedroom linen weekly—the top sheet moving to the bottom and the bottom sheet getting washed. She did three loads of laundry a week in the gas-powered wringer washing machine, which had an exhaust vent through the floor in the original house. In the new house the washing machine was located in the enclosed back porch, with the exhaust vented through a pipe in the wall. Diane also worked in the store and when she was old enough, she was awarded the assistant postmaster position.

Art remembered working and working hard, starting at about age eight. The boys' chores included dispensing fuel to boats from the marine gas station on the wharf, fixing machinery, helping in the fish camp unloading and weighing the spring and coho salmon and icing them in large fish boxes, which were then shipped off to Victoria. Many times they iced long into the night, weighing in as much as 30,000 pounds (13,600 kg) of fish. On one particular night, they iced close to 75,000 pounds (34,000 kg) of salmon!

Hugh remembers at age six fuelling up the fishboats, at age eight signing papers and by age ten working in the fish camp buying fish. His inquisitive mind came up with an easier, less work-intensive system for the weighing and icing process the fish went through in preparation for shipping. As a young boy, on his own initiative, he placed an order for the wood and materials needed to make a stand for the fish scale. Canadian Fishing Company supplied and shipped the wood free of charge from Vancouver on one of its packers, although Ivan first queried Hugh on what it was for. Originally, the large scale sat on the floor and the fish had to be pitchforked onto the scale and then again into the fish box. When the wood arrived, Hugh built a stand for the scale to sit on, so all they had to do was pitch the fish up onto the scale, weigh them and then open a door and let the fish slide down into the fish box. It was a vast improvement over the way they had been doing the work, and they didn't have to handle the fish as much.

The boys also worked in the store with their mother and sisters.

Mabel worked at the main counter of the store and did the paperwork, tallying up what the fishermen owed and were owed, and kept records of the people their business had extended credit to. Nada, being the eldest girl, was the first daughter to help her mom in the store. As Patsy got older she kept the books for the family business when Ivan and Mabel were away. In 1952 Patsy and Hugh were both sworn in as assistant postmasters by Les Hammer, postmaster of Port Alberni, who was also a long-time friend of Ivan's. Les went on to become the mayor of Port Alberni.

Although there were earlier, larger versions, starting in the early 1940s there was a BC Telephone Company phone at the Clarke store. Their ring was two short and three long. The store phone was on a party line and folks had to be careful what they said as they could never be sure who might be eavesdropping on the other end. As he had the only phone for miles around, Ivan probably charged people to use it, just as he had for his telegraph service. Starting in the 1960s, communication with the fishboats and other marine traffic was by VHF radio. It was not until August 1997, long after Ivan had retired, that BC Tel would install the first telephone system in the village at Hot Springs Cove.

School Developments

In 1960, Sydney Inlet School changed its name to Hot Springs School. The same year, the school was forced to close its doors when the Clarke children completed their education.

The Sydney Inlet School closed in 1960. A former floating bunkhouse, the school building also hosted community meetings and the occasional religious service when the Messenger III, the mission boat of the Shantymen's Christian Association, came to the cove. Harold Peters (left) and Rev. Percy Wills are shown standing on deck. Maritime Museum of BC, 990.009.0017

The one-room Sydney Inlet School had also functioned as the community hall, as well as a meeting place at election time for political discussions. When the Shantymen's Christian Association's mission boat, the 45-foot *Messenger III* visited the cove, the school was used for services, singsongs and showing travelogue movies. The Shantymen's Association still exists as SCA International, a Toronto-based evangelical mission focused on the more remote parts of Canada. It was started on the west coast of Vancouver Island in 1930 when Reverend Percy E. Wills began work as their missionary, travelling up and down the west coast in the 10-hp launch, SCA.

Hugh had a humorous story about Reverend Wills. Hugh was helping a friend build a cabin on his open fishboat. The friend had decided to go up and watch the travel movies while Hugh worked on the boat's cabin. When it was too dark to continue working, Hugh walked up the gangplank and thought he saw his friend walking down, so he blurted out, "Where have you been? I could have used your help," with a cuss word thrown in. It turned out not to be his friend, but Reverend Wills, who scolded Hugh and told him he was too young to leave the Bible.

Schoolteacher Ivy Youell would give religion classes on Sundays, which the Clarke family attended. Hugh said that one particular Sunday, Mrs. Youell said something that offended Ivan, quite possibly about him smoking in the schoolhouse, and he turned and said, "Come on boys, we are out of here," and out went Ivan and all his sons. It's uncertain if they attended religion classes after that, but Hugh said that on the Monday, it was still school as usual for the children.

In 1953, there were 12 students attending Sydney Inlet School, the majority of them being Clarkes. Early on, the Florence Nightingale Chapter of the Imperial Order of the Daughters of the Empire (IODE), a women's charitable organization, adopted the school. This entailed supplying the school with much-needed items that the Ministry of Education did not provide, such as library books, calendars, a Viewmaster, Christmas packages and more. The organization had many members who were wives of tugboat captains and other marine workers, some of them wives of Ivan's former co-workers, who made sure the students at Sydney Inlet School were well taken care of.

In 1955, Island Tug & Barge tugboat captain William R. Roskelley's wife, Winnifred, at that time the chapter's education secretary, supplied a picture of Queen Elizabeth for the school, followed later with one of the Duke of Edinburgh. The IODE continued to send books, magazines, Easter and Christmas gifts to their adopted school at least until the end of the 1950s.

Mrs. Youell taught at the school from 1946 to 1957.

Homebodies

Ivan revealed to his son Raymond, many years later, that he kept Mabel "barefoot and pregnant" so she would not leave him. In reality, in the beginning, Ivan and Mabel hardly ever ventured together too far from the cove. Trips away—much less family trips to Victoria—were few and far between. When any of the Clarke children did visit Victoria, it probably included a visit to see their uncle Hugh at his dentist office in the Central Building on View Street for a checkup. It must have been bad enough having an uncle who was the Victoria School District dentist, but their uncle Albert was also a dentist in Victoria.

In their first 20 years of marriage, Ivan and Mabel took only two extended vacations. They flew twice to Honolulu, 18 months apart, and both times were very happy to return to their Hot Springs Cove home. One of my older Elworthy cousins once told me, "The difference between going on a vacation and going on holidays is that when you go on vacation, you leave your kids at home." Ivan would occasionally leave the cove and head down to Victoria for business and personal reasons. He would fly down to Port Alberni where he kept his burgundy 1962 Pontiac two-door hardtop, which he would then drive down the island. When he moved to Victoria years later, the car still looked like it was new.

Once a week, a list was made for the Liquor Control Board's mail-order department on East Hastings Street in Vancouver for the adults at the cove. This would be sent down on the North Arm Transport packer or sometimes it would be sent by registered mail, and about a week later the order would be delivered by a returning North Arm packer and be distributed between family members, the other fish camps and fishermen as per their requests. Alcohol consumption and everything related to it was definitely a personal problem for Ivan and some of the others at Hot Springs Cove. He had started drinking and smoking years earlier, at least by the time he was working on the tugs.

Even before Ivan moved to the cove, occasionally during bad storms, American boats would sneak into the harbour and drop anchor. Once Ivan

Liquor was ordered for the cove on a weekly basis from the Liquor Control Board in Vancouver. Alcohol consumption would prove to be a problem for many residents at Hot Springs Cove. Courtesy of Ron Leith Auctions Inc.

was there, he was not about to let any boat wallow out in the Pacific during a storm. Should Fisheries happen upon these boats, their way of thinking was that if their Fisheries boat could make it to the cove during the storm, it was not too rough to send the American boats back out again. If the Americans were lucky when the Fisheries boat came in to chase them away, Ivan would start drinking with the Fisheries officers, and soon enough they would just leave the American boats alone.

One newspaper story involving Fisheries reported that many years earlier, the 149-foot salvage tug SS *William T. Jolliffe*, which was engaged in Fisheries protection work, came into Refuge Cove and found a number of American craft sheltering.

That night the wind was blowing hard and there were snow squalls, but the *Jolliffe* hoisted anchor and headed out into the blow. Consequently, with bad grace, the Americans hoisted their hooks and also headed out into it. After motoring around for some hours the tug came back into her mooring, followed by the drenched and disgusted Americans. The next morning, the tug struck out again with the Americans trailing along. If they had not followed, the Dominion Government boat would have had a case against them for using a British harbour.

When the salvage tug was built in 1885, in South Shields, Durham, England, it was touted as being the world's most powerful tug. The *William T. Jolliffe* was renamed the *Salvage Chief* when it was purchased by the Pacific Salvage Company in Victoria in 1924.

Earlier Business Attempts:
Land, Water Rights Claimed

B usiness interests through the years could have resulted in the development of a hotel and summer resort or a sanitarium at what is now Hot
Springs Cove. Even Ivan originally would have liked to open a health resort
there. As noted earlier, though, by the time he decided to acquire land at what
was then known as Refuge Cove, someone had already beaten him to the
actual lot the hot springs were located on. (See first mention of Robert Wyllie in chapter 1.)

In terms of land opportunities at the cove earlier in the twentieth century, William Gibson of the powerful Gibson family lumber barons had
already been Crown granted part of Lots 1371 and 1372, which were rough
survey-staked in 1912. These are the lots that would capture Ivan's interest in
1933. In the August 12, 1912, *British Columbia Gazette* on page 7702, the body
of the Gibson announcement reads:

ALBERNI LAND DISTRICT
DISTRICT OF CLAYOQUOT

Take notice that I, William Gibson, of Vancouver, B.C., Miner, intend
to apply for permission to purchase the following described lands:

Commencing at a post in the north-east corner of Lot 486, Clayoquot District; thence north along the shore-line to Indian Reserve;
thence west along south boundary of Indian Reserve to the southwest corner thereof; thence north along the west boundary of said
Indian Reserve 30 chains; Thence east along the northern boundary
of said Indian Reserve to the shore-line; thence along the shore-line
northerly 30 chains; thence west to the shore-line of Refuge Cove;
thence southerly along the shore-line 80 chains; thence east 20 chains
to the point of commencement. [A chain is 20 metres.]

The Gibson grant of Lot 1372 was confirmed on October 9, 1913, but it
eventually reverted back to the Crown. Similarly, Lot 1371 was Crown granted
to Gibson on April 3, 1914, and reverted back to the Crown on September 9,
1931.

Water Rights

As for the hot springs themselves, William M. Brewer, a well-known mining
engineer in Victoria, owned the water rights to them in the late 1800s. He estimated the rate of flow to be 100,000 gallons of water per day. In 1898, he sent a
sample of the water to the Geological Survey of Canada laboratory in Ottawa
for analysis by Chief Chemist Frank G. Wait. The analysis came back showing
the water was apparently lacking the minor mineral constituents to which the
therapeutic value of mineral waters were commonly ascribed, hence it had no
medicinal or therapeutic value.

Even with that knowledge, Brewer regularly ran the following announcement, which appeared in the *Daily Colonist* in the last half of 1899. The same
announcement was also found under "Land Notices" in the *British Columbia
Gazette*, September 7, 1899, page 1526, with the exception that it was for 160
acres (65 hectares) and Brewer and his associates were going to apply within
30 days.

Notice of Application

The undersigned will apply within 60 days of date, to the Chief Commissioner of Lands and Works at Victoria, BC, for permission to pur-

chase or lease 100 acres of land more or less, which forms the point known as Sharp Point, lying between Refuge Cove and Sydney Inlet, on the west coast of Vancouver Island. The line of said land to commence at a certain post set up the 19th day of June, 1899, on the west shore of Sharp Point, thence 20 chains east, thence following the shore line southerly around the Point, and northerly back to place of commencement, at said post.

It was signed by Brewer, J. Ringlund, S. Obinger, K. Peterson and J. A. Drinkwater.

The following is part of Brewer's letter of September 14, 1899, to the chief commissioner of lands and works in Victoria, outlining plans for a hotel and summer resort:

On behalf of the Messers. J. Ringlund, K. Peterson, S. Obinger, J. A. Drinkwater and myself, I beg to make application for permission to purchase or lease 160 acres of land more or less, on the West Coast of Vancouver Island...

The provisions of said Section 30 have been complied with; the initial post was erected on the 19th day of June 1899, and notice of application was advertised in the BC Gazette of 10th August 1899, notice was also posted at the Government Office, Alberni, BC on 25th July 1899.

The purpose for which the applicants require the said land is for a site for a hotel and summer resort, and the amount of land applied for is required in order to enable them to have a proper land place for the erection of their wharves, &c., and also to enable the applicants to have sufficient ground to make the place attractive for people who come to the hotel. I may state also that from personal examination of the land, I know that it is all rocky, with scrub timber, and is of no value whatever for agricultural purposes.

I enclose a photograph of the land, which will serve to give some idea of [its] topography.

It was signed by Brewer, "for self and as Agent" for Ringland, Peterson, Obinger and Drinkwater.

Just over two months later at the Executive Council Chamber in Victoria, an order-in-council was approved granting a lease to Brewer and company to the Sharp Point land. It read in part:

His Honour the Lieutenant Governor of British Columbia and with the advice of the Executive Council doth order as follows:

That a lease be granted to Messrs: J. Ringland, K. Peterson, S. Obinger, J.A. Drinkwater and W.M. Brewer of 160 acres [65 hectares] of land at Sharp Point, lying between Refuge Cove and Sydney Inlet on the West Coast of Vancouver Island, as a site for a hotel and summer resort, for a term of twenty-one years, at an annual rental of twenty-five cents per acre [$40 per year in 1899 or about $1,200 in 2019].

In January 1898, Peterson, Drinkwater and Obinger were noted under the "Personal" column of the *Daily Colonist* as being among the latest arrivals at the Queens Hotel in Victoria and were said to be all mining men from Clayoquot. But with all their lease paperwork in place, one can only assume that Brewer and his consortium were unable to raise the capital money needed to see their hotel and summer resort a reality, and their lease reverted back to the Crown.

New Application

Then, in the December 7, 1905, edition of the *British Columbia Gazette*, on page 2724, W. B. Garrard and S. R. Ramsay posted the following announcement.

Notice is hereby given that, 60 days after this date, we intend applying to the Chief Commissioner of Lands and Works for permission to purchase the following lands, situate[d] in Clayoquot District on that neck of land between Sydney Inlet and Refuge Cove known as Sharp Point: —Starting from a point marked "S.W. corner post" near the west extremity of Sharp Point; thence 10 chains east; thence 20 chains north; thence 10 chains west and back to the point of commencement, being an area of 20 acres more or less.

The November 11, 1906, Victoria *Daily Colonist* included an article out of Nanaimo written about a William Garrard, who was a miner from Clayoquot, telling of a remarkable hot spring that he had located about six months earlier. It is interesting to note in the six years between William M. Brewer having had the water analyzed and Garrard's remarkable find, the water was now of high medicinal value. The article read:

Prospectors Discover Medicinal Water
Bubbling Out of the Ground

Nanaimo, Nov. 10.—(Special)—E. B. Gerrard [*sic*], of Clayoquot, is in the city. He tells of the discovery of a remarkable hot spring which he and a number of associates have discovered in that vicinity, and which may ultimately lead to the erection of a sanitorium on the west coast. Those interested in the discovery are W.B. Ramsay, B. Markland of New Westminster, and Mr. Gerrard. While prospecting some time ago at Sharps Inlet, Sydney Point [*sic*], the party came across the hot spring, which was bubbling out of the ground in large quantities. A clinical thermometer, placed in the spring, registered 125 degrees [Fahrenheit]. Samples of the water were taken and submitted [for] analysis, with the result that the water is proven to be of high medicinal value, the chief ingredients of which are sodium and sulphur. As the springs are within a stone's throw of salt water, and the surroundings most picturesque, the location is an ideal one for the erection of a sanitarium. The discoverers are taking the necessary steps to claim their find, and a large area of land adjoining. Already they have been made substantial offers for the spring, which they have declined.

Six months later, in the May 10, 1907, Victoria *Daily Colonist* there was a follow-up article about William Garrard, who was proposing the idea of building and conducting a hot springs sanitarium there.

Site For Sanitarium On The West Coast Hot Springs Location
on Sharp's Point May Soon be Utilized

A joint stock company is to be organized for the purpose of building and conducting a hot springs sanitarium on the west coast of Vancouver

Island. W. B. Garrard, who located the springs about a year ago, was to the city yesterday, a guest at the Victoria Hotel, and he left this morning for Vancouver, where he will consult others interested with him in the ownership of the location.

The springs are from a rock about a hundred yards from the extremity of Shap [sic] Point, which is 30 miles north of Clayoquot, and is between Sidney Inlet and Refuge Cove. There is at present no landing place there for steamers.

The water, which at its source has a temperature of 125 degrees [Fahrenheit], was discovered many years ago by Indians and used by them for healing purposes. A party of prospectors came upon the scene one day, and later reported it to Mr. Garrard, who with Robert Ramsey was engaged in timber cruising. He staked out 20 acres of land around the springs, and afterwards secured a government lease of the water rights. He says the water has the odor of sulphur, but an analysis proved that sodium was the principal component part. When cool it tastes something like rain water. There is a sufficient supply in sight to fill a four-inch pipe laid at a one-in-ten grade.

As a site for a sanitarium Sharp Point has something unique in the way of scenery. There is nothing pastoral in the surroundings, but there are grand snow-capped mountains in the background and high, rugged rocks in front, and on either side against which the full force of the Pacific waves have play. There is no obstacle, except the range of vision, to a view straight across the ocean, and all the C. P. R. Oriental liners can be seen coming and going.

Mr. Garrard believes, from what he has learned of cures among the Indians who used the springs, that there is wonderful healing power in the water, and that a sanitarium with such a unique location and so much to recommend it to people in search of health and wild scenery, would easily become a paying proposition. He has had offers for the property, but none of these have been high enough to cause him to believe that he and those interested with him in the ownership would profit as much by selling out as they would by engaging in business for themselves.

On April 27, 1908, Garrard and Ramsay were Crown land granted Clayoquot District Lot 697 (which was a portion of Clayoquot District Lot 486), but must not have gathered the interest and capital that they had hoped for with their sanitarium plans, as they seemed to have just sat on their land grant and finally let their land revert back to the Crown in October 1921, probably by defaulting on their payments for it.

Samuel Robert Ramsay (also spelled Ramsey) may well have been the namesake for the Ramsay Hot Springs, although as mentioned earlier, the origin of the name remains unclear. In about 1912, Walter Wallace Rhodes, a mining engineer from California living in Tofino, made an application for the water rights of the hot springs, but he did not make good with his claim either. In the Dominion Government Summary Report of the Geological Survey Department of Mines of 1913, as part of his four-page report on the hot springs, Charles Horace Clapp reported that:

The prospective value of hot mineral waters appeared to be speculative as the location of a popular pleasure resort. The Sharp Point water is apparently lacking, or nearly so, in most of those minor constituents like bromine, iodine, sulphur, lithium, barium, strontium, and iron, to which the therapeutic value of mineral waters is commonly ascribed; but...the water was similar in its percentage composition to the Rotorua geyser waters [in New Zealand], which are supposed to have great healing qualities.

The same report noted that "except for the wet climate, the Sharp Point spring is apparently favourably located for a summer resort, which would certainly be cool and afford a variety of ocean and mountain scenery and an abundance of out-of-door activities."

Ivan Arrives

Ivan arrived on the scene in 1933, six years after the Crown had granted Robert W. Wyllie of Vancouver the 20 acres (8 hectares) that made up Clayoquot Land District Lot 697, including the land the hot springs were on, for $200. On November 14, 1952, when Wyllie was living in Toronto, the Crown granted him Clayoquot Land District Lot 486, a further 45 acres (18 hectares) for $723. This land surrounded his Lot 697, and also bordered on Ivan's property. Wyllie also owned an old mine up Stewardson Inlet, where Ivan salvaged building materials from. Wyllie, though, seems to have kept away from his land assets.

Ivan's friend Major George Nicholson used to say, "The Springs are wholly undeveloped; free for all to enjoy and worth a million if they were handy and accessible by road, which of course they never will be."

Since Ivan's original dream was to build a health resort at the cove, surely over the years he must have tried to acquire District Lot 697 from Robert Wyllie. With money in his own family, Wyllie must have had his own plans for the hot springs when he decided to also acquire District Lot 486. But Lot 486 was of no value to Ivan for a health resort without owning Lot 697, which contained the hot springs. Even if he had managed to acquire both of Wyllie's lots, he would have also needed to secure a government lease of the water rights to the hot spring.

Not long after learning about Wyllie's second land grant in 1952, Ivan and Mabel started to think about donating some of their land to the people of British Columbia for park purposes. When Ivan and Mabel did finally donate the land, that would have ended any development plans that Robert had for his hot springs, as any improvements he tried to make would have meant having to use the government wharf at Ivan's operation, crossing Ivan's land and walking through the new provincial park to both access his hot springs and get his supplies in.

CHAPTER 9

Parkland Donation:
Ivan and Mabel's Gift

On November 26, 1953, in Victoria, Major George Nicholson, on behalf of Ivan and Mabel Clarke, offered 25 acres (10 hectares) of land at Hot Springs Cove to the people of British Columbia to be used as parkland. The *Daily Colonist* mentioned that the proposed park would contain "hot sulphur springs, a waterfall and swimming pool" and went on to say that the hot springs would have an uninterrupted view of the Pacific ocean. In reality, the hot springs themselves and the waterfall were on privately owned land, which was not owned by Ivan.

Along with the Clarkes' offer, Ivan suggested the name "Maquinna Park" after Mowachaht chief Maquinna and the ss *Princess Maquinna*, which had faithfully serviced Hot Springs Cove for many years. The government said that the name would be considered and provisionally accepted the offer. Thanks were also given to the Clarke family for their generous gift to the people of BC. The government surveyors eventually came up and Hugh helped them with the survey, marking off the land that was now to become part of the park.

As far as the swimming pool is concerned, it's uncertain if that referred to a big wooden bathtub of Ivan's or even if that was still around then. Ivan might or might not have received permission from Robert Wyllie to make some improvements at the hot springs, but in the early 1940s he would get any fishermen heading out on the trail to the hot springs to carry along one long board. After some time, he had enough boards out at the springs to build a wooden bathtub about 5 feet wide, 11 feet long and 3 feet high (1.5×3.3×1 m), on the south side of the stream above the waterfalls. At the end of the tub, there was a narrow boardwalk that divided the bathtub from a good-sized change room that he also built—complete with inside benches—overlooking the ocean. The change room was a vast improvement over having to change behind a handy shrub or salal bush. The tub was filled by a 2-inch (5-cm) steel pipe that could be swung out of the way when the tub was full.

30.7 Acres

In November 1954, a year after making their offer, Ivan and Mabel were down in Victoria to discuss with government officials the turning over of what had now grown to 30.7 acres (12.4 hectares) of their land to the people of British Columbia for park purposes.

The parcel of land straddled Openit Peninsula with sea frontages on the Hot Springs Cove west side and the Sydney Inlet east side, just north of the hot springs, but did not include the land that the actual hot springs themselves were on. The southern line of the new park was the northern boundary of Lot 486. Then from the southwest corner of Ahousaht Reserve No. 27, north, almost to Ivan's settlement and then heading slightly southwest toward the shore of Hot Springs Cove. This last particular line had been moved somewhat northward to enlarge the park from the original 25 acres to 30.7 acres (10 to 12.4 hectares). Ivan made sure that any possible landing place for small craft on the Hot Springs Cove side had been included in the new park, and that it would not be possible for a future private owner of Lot 1372 to build a wharf or float on that part of the shoreline. (See drawing of Lot A on Clayoquot Land District Lot 1372 on opposite page.)

On November 24, 1954, the 30.7-acre site was formally handed over to the people of British Columbia in care of the provincial government for development as a park. Ivan signed the official documents and was witnessed by George Nicholson, who had been associated with Ivan in negotiations of the transfer. The park was not officially named until after it had been gazetted, which took about a month, after which Ivan's suggested name was used and it became Maquinna Provincial Park.

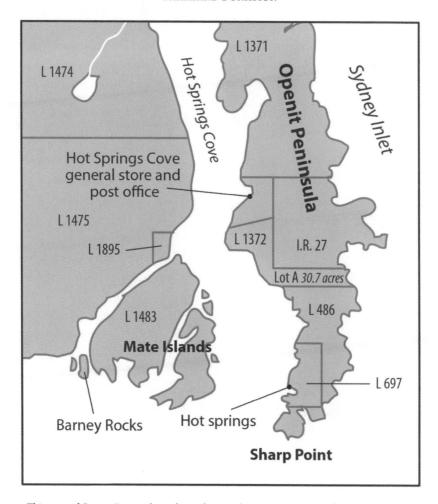

This map of Openit Peninsula in the mid-1950s shows Ivan and Mabel's parkland donation of 30.7 acres, identified as Lot A. Ahousaht First Nation Openit No. 27 Reserve is just to the north of the donation. Lots 486 and 697, owned by Robert Wyllie, were later purchased by the provincial government and added to the park. Royal BC Museum and Archives, GR-1614.23.17, Box 23

On December 8, 1954, the last official papers were signed and Ivan and Mabel left a wonderful legacy to the people of British Columbia. Maquinna Provincial Park was officially established by order-in-council on January 7, 1955. Although the land was in Ivan's name, it was donated by both Ivan and Mabel. It was their intention that the people of British Columbia would forever have free land access through the new park to the hot springs. Just to make it official, the government paid Ivan and Mabel one dollar to complete the transaction. This still left them 17.5 acres (7.1 hectares) of the original Crown Land Grant Lot 1372 surrounding their operation and wharves.

In the park, there was a raised-letter bronze plaque reading:

Province of British Columbia, Maquinna Provincial Park, Established January 7, 1955. The land originally comprising the park was donated to the people of British Columbia through the generosity of Ivan H. Clarke a long time resident of Hot Springs Cove.

Apparently, the first plaque eventually disappeared and a second one was cast, which now sits on a low slate cairn beside the start of the boardwalk.

Ivan received a letter at Hot Springs Cove dated August 29, 1960, sent to him from the minister of recreation and conservation in Victoria, saying:

Dear Mr. Clark [sic]:

I hope that you will be pleased to receive the enclosed booklets. They are a further testimony to the gratitude felt by the people of British Columbia for the generous gift of land you made to them for park purposes. Yours will be a gift that will be enjoyed by succeeding generations of British Columbians, and this small testimonial to your generosity is another way of saying thank you from Government of the Province of British Columbia. Should you require further copies, please do not hesitate to write me.

Yours very truly,

Earle C. Westward, Minister

Life Goes On at the Cove

Around the time of the parkland donation, there were just under one hundred people living at Hot Springs Cove. The 1955 *Victoria City and Vancouver Island Directory* describes Hot Springs Cove as "P[ost] O[ffice] 25 miles

By the time of the parkland donation in 1954, Ivan's operation included, from left to right, the school, teacher's residence, a glass-roofed workshop, family home (built with materials from the bunkhouse barge), general store, a workshop built by his son Hugh and a restaurant (not pictured). Two water towers are visible in the background, behind the house. Major George Nicholson Collection/Ken Gibson Collection

north of Clayoquot on west coast of Vancouver Island served by BC Coast Steamships Service and Pacific Western Airlines. (Formerly Refuge Cove)." Twenty-seven inhabitants—not including wives and children—were listed.

In other events at the cove, on March 25, 1955, the *Daily Colonist* reported that rainmaking machines were operating on the west coast of Vancouver Island.

Rain making machines are now operating on the west coast of Vancouver Island, but B.C. Power Commission officials are not speculating as to whether or not .56 inches of precipitation on Monday and .25 inches on Tuesday are directly attributed to use of the machines.

"We just can't tell until they have operated over a period of several months," they said yesterday.

They argue that the rain might have fallen over Campbell River watershed in any event.

John Walser, meteorologist of North West Weather Consultants, returned to Victoria yesterday and reported that silver iodide generating machines have been set up at Ucluelet, Tofino, Hot Springs Cove, Gold River, Bligh Island in Nootka Sound...

Machines at Ucluelet, Tofino and Hot Springs Cove have been in operation since March 14, but because wind and cloud conditions have not yet been suitable the other generators have not operated.

Walser, a full-time meteorologist who was on a one-year contract, had established headquarters in Victoria. He was in direct contact with the weather office in Victoria and was setting up communications with the office in Port Alberni. It was not necessary that all of the rain machines operated at the same time. Ivan Clarke and the other west coast operators received their instructions according to the weather and wind conditions in their area.

Christmas at the Cove

Over the years, Christmas at Hot Springs Cove had become a big, festive annual event. The Clarkes celebrated with their Nuu-chah-nulth and multicultural fishermen friends.

Around the third week of December, Santa Claus would arrive by sea to some 20 west coast Vancouver Island communities, fishing villages and logging ports as the CPR BC Coast Service motor vessel *Princess of Alberni* made her pre-Christmas rounds. The *Princess of Alberni* had gone into west coast service in 1953, but the tradition of the west coast Santa Claus sailings had been started toward the end of the 1800s by the Union Steamship Company's 165-foot ship SS *Tees*, built in 1893, and was continued into the first half of the 1900s by the *Princess Maquinna*. Captain Edward Gillam, master of the SS *Tees* and then of the SS *Princess Maquinna*, played a very convincing Santa Claus until his accidental death in 1929.

The annual expedition of the ship was a huge event for the isolated residents, more eagerly anticipated than all the regularly-scheduled stops, as the cargo on this trip contained holiday gifts and mail. All the BC Coast Service west coast scheduled stops were honoured if the weather conditions permitted and if there was cargo aboard for that particular stop. Living in a protected cove, and having a father who ran the only store and post office for miles around, there's no doubt the children at Hot Springs Cove were among those that Santa Claus always found his way to by sea. On March 18, 1956, the *Daily Colonist* carried the following article.

They Had 99 For Dinner At Christmas

A dinner that would make the average housewife go strike if she had to prepare it, was served last Christmas by Mr. and Mrs. Ivan H. Clarke, who operate a general store at Hot Springs Cove on the west coast of Vancouver Island. They were assisted by their eight children, the local school teacher, Mrs. Ivy M. Youell, her husband, and several fishermen who made the cove their headquarters.

Sixty-six people sat down to dinner Christmas Day and 33 the day after. Places were set for 100 and the only reason they didn't all sit together, was because a southeast gale prevented the 33, who live on the opposite side of the cove, from crossing over in their boats.

Of the 99 who partook of the Clarke's hospitality, 25 were white people and the remainder Indians, about half of them children. Actually, that number accounts for the cove's total population. The dinner is an annual event.

It was served in the large, glassed-in veranda of the Clarke residence, which was decorated with festoons of greenery and colored paper. Tables and chairs were borrowed from the schoolhouse and church.

The eight 16-pound turkeys were cooked in relays—some the day before—in two ordinary size household ranges.

So much stuffing was required that it had to be mixed in a galvanized iron washtub, and there was almost that much gravy.

Other items that went to make up the menu included two gallons of cranberry sauce, 20 loaves of bread, a sack of potatoes and several crates of cauliflower and other vegetables.

For dessert there was plum pudding, 20 homemade apple pies, 10 boxes of Japanese oranges, a whole bunch of bananas and a case each of fresh apples and pears. The tables were heaped with cakes, cookies, candies, nuts and raisins. Everybody received bon bons and other novelties; all wore paper hats and between them they consumed ten dozen bottles of pop.

All received a gift from three heavily laden Christmas trees and there was also a five-foot stocking filled with prizes for the kiddies.

The dinner started with Mr. Youell asking God's Blessing and finished up by Chief Benedict Andrews and George Sye, on behalf

Seasons Greetings

IVAN & MABEL CLARKE & FAMILY

HOT SPRINGS COVE, B.C.

Christmas was a much-anticipated, festive affair at Hot Springs Cove, complete with a visit from Santa by boat. In 1955, ninety-nine guests gathered at the Clarkes' for Christmas dinner. Major George Nicholson Collection/Ken Gibson Collection

of the Indians, thanking the Clarke family in appropriate speeches. Games were played afterwards and everyone danced to the rhythm of Indian drums.

Not forgotten was a lone Catholic priest, one [other] family and about 30 Indians, who live at Hesquiat, which is 12 miles further up-coast, but separated from the cove by a very rough stretch of water.

Anticipating bad weather at this time of year, Mr. Clarke sent them up two turkeys also, along with all the trimmings necessary for their Christmas dinner.

Ivan became used to having large gatherings of people for Christmas when he was growing up. The adults in the house would decorate the tree on Christmas Eve. His father would light the candles in small metal holders, clipped like clothes pegs to the branches. When the decorating was finished, the children would be allowed a quick look at the presents under the tree before they were sent upstairs to bed, and his father would then snuff out the candles. It was a wonder that more fires didn't start from the open flames among the greenery, but his father never left the candles burning for very long. Along with the ornaments and decorations, each branch would also be laden with the traditional popcorn and candy, of which the tree would be stripped clean by Ivan and his siblings on Christmas day.

About five o'clock on Christmas morning, all the children would be sitting two together in their night clothes on the steep stairs coming down from their bedrooms, waiting for their father to unlock the sitting room door. He would arise about six and all the children would troop in. It was wonderful for the children as they could always count on Santa to bring them the gifts that they wanted. Six years before Ivan was born, Santa even brought the children a baby brother for Christmas, and six years before that, Santa brought a baby brother as an early Christmas present on December 23.

At dinner time, the extended family, including Ivan's older married siblings and their small families, would sit down at a long table running the length of their kitchen, their father at one end and their mother presiding at the other end. Their father would carve the turkey and their mother would carve the goose. They also had potatoes, carrots, greens and other vegetables grown in their garden. If they could manage it after the main course, there was a big plum pudding for dessert. It was a great dinner enjoyed by all!

Afterwards, the children would play with their toys and later everybody would gather and sing around the organ. They'd occasionally sing popular music of the day, but mostly just hymns, as proper Methodists did. And then there would be games like Post Office (the board/acting game, not the kissing game), bean-bag toss through the open mouth of a cardboard figure, forfeits (a word action game) and charades. There was no dancing or playing cards, as that was not thought proper in the family. A special traditional family ceremony held at the end of the day was having their father measure each child to see how much they had grown in the past year and marking their height on the pantry doorjamb. Ivan had the same tradition with his children when they were growing up, except he did it right before school started in September.

One Boxing Day in the early 1960s, I remember Ivan, my grandfather, showing up at our door unexpectedly. We never knew when he was going to appear; it was always a surprise. Before he left he drove me to the corner store and bought me any one toy that I wanted, and made sure that the required batteries were purchased also.

Planes and a Shipwreck

Ivan and the boys were always checking the skies overhead for airplanes. Plane spotting and identification was an important piece of the puzzle on the west coast during the Cold War, mainly after the death of Soviet leader Joseph Stalin in March 1953 until the Cuban Missile Crisis in 1962. The "JULIETT ECHO 42 BLACK" call sign and observation post was established December 2, 1952. Chief Observer Ivan Clarke, and his five sons (Raymond was married and living in Victoria by then) were well trained in the art of plane spotting, so they could send Aircraft Flash Calls to a filter centre, which amassed a thick field report from Hot Springs Cove. While it was in operation, the field report read like a best seller. The post was visited by nearly every officer in the detachment. One call a day from "JULIETT ECHO 42 BLACK" was the target number from the filter centre in 1957.

Hugh still has his framed certificate hanging on his living room wall. It is worded: "Presented to: Hugh Clarke in appreciation of valuable service rendered as a member of the Ground Observer Corps., of the Royal Canadian Air Force" and dated June 1, 1960, Ottawa, Ontario, signed by Hugh Campbell, Air Marshall, Chief of the Air Staff.

Around this time, a long-lost shipwreck brought visitors to nearby Sydney Inlet.

In 1957, a party headed by Dr. George W. Cotterell from Portland, Oregon, was trying to find the 269-ton fur-trader vessel *Tonquin*, captained by Jonathon Thorn, which had been sunk in 1811 at Wickaninnish Island near Tofino. It had been blown up by its lone remaining crew member to prevent it from being captured by the local Indigenous people, who had ambushed and killed the rest of the crew the day before.

The search had to be abandoned due to bad weather, but working with information given to the group by John Campbell, an elderly member of the Ahousaht First Nation, they discovered what—after many more years of further research—turned out to be the British East Indiaman ship *Lord Western*, which ran aground on December 4, 1853. It had been built in Scotland, with hardwoods from Southeast Asia, and launched on March 5, 1840. Its most notable features include a three-masted barque with square rigging, a figurehead carved in the shape of a man and a copper bottom.

It was one of the first ships to export products from Vancouver Island and its cargo included Douglas fir pilings, squared timbers and salted salmon. Its final destination was San Francisco. The building boom in San Francisco, caused by the gold rush, had made lumber for houses, docks and piers a valuable commodity. The Ahousaht people had saved the crew after the ship had foundered. Hudson's Bay Company records from that time showed that Governor James Douglas had a local boat head up the coast to pick up any survivors. Although much of the ship was dispersed over the sloping ocean floor, potions of the ship, such as the inner hull, were still intact and visible. In total, the shipwreck measured approximately 125 feet by 40 feet (38×12 m). The bow laid in about 34 feet (10.5 metres) of water, while the stern laid in about 72 feet (22 metres) of water. Portions of mahogany and teak, copper sheathing, brass rivets, and even a canon were amongst some of the material salvaged from the wreck, much of which was turned over to Ivan as the deputy receiver of wrecks. Ivan's superior, Gerald A. Yardley, arranged for a transport department vessel to take all the artifacts to Victoria.

The Royal Canadian Navy (RCN) arrived on the scene in 1959 with the 147-foot 4-inch minesweeper HMCS *James Bay* and the naval auxiliary vessel, the 168-foot *Laymore*. They carried a team from the RCN diving school. The Navy divers returned in 1960, with the minesweeper and diver tender the HMCS *Mirimichi* and were able to retrieve an anchor, a windlass, a bronze gudgeon, copper sheathing, rivets, a capstan and the copper penny placed under the main mast for good luck during construction.

In 1988, a grant of $12,600 was given to the Underwater Archeological Society of BC from the British Columbia Heritage Trust for the purpose of surveying and mapping the ship wreck at the bottom of Adventure Cove. A captain's telescope and a Chinese ceramic bowl were two of the items that were discovered in the survey. *Lord Western* is the oldest known shipwreck discovered to date on the west coast of Vancouver Island. It is now a registered provincial historic site.

CHAPTER 10

Getting There:
Access Improves

The most obvious change to Hot Springs Cove over the years has been access. Today we can drive our vehicles to Tofino from Port Alberni and take a boat or float plane to Hot Springs Cove. But it was only in August 1959 that the early version of that road between the Tofino area and Port Alberni, a long-awaited logging road winding through the mountains via Long Beach and Kennedy Lake, was finished.

Back on Sunday, April 14, 1912, the Victoria *Daily Colonist* reported:

The Vancouver Island Development League is trying to remedy this by pressing for an automobile road from Alberni via the north side of Sproat Lake, halfway up Taylor River, turn south over the summit to Elk River thence via Kennedy Lake to Ucluelet, Long Beach and Clayoquot townsite, now known as Tofino. In length, this would be about 60 miles from Alberni to Long Beach.

The article also reported that the Department of Works was to complete a survey that summer for an automobile road from Sproat Lake to Ucluelet. The road from Tofino to Long Beach would be completed, as well as a road from Long Beach to the Ucluelet wharf.

On November 9, 1929, the *Daily Colonist* published a lengthy article titled "Clayoquot Seeks Road Connection" urging the Public Works Department to build a road along the west coast of Vancouver Island from Long Beach to Sproat Lake. The article further noted that the Clayoquot Sound Conservative Association, Tofino Good Roads League, cannery operators, and various miners, lumbermen and fishermen were all advocating for this road, citing it as crucial to the future industrial development of the area. Mentioned also were all the isolated settlements and businesses that would benefit by a road providing daily access and communication with Port Alberni. A paragraph was dedicated to Refuge Cove.

> In Refuge Cove is the famous West Coast hot spring, the rendezvous of fishermen in the Summer. Slightly sulphurous, the spring supplies a waterfall with several pools below for bathing. Many suffering from rheumatism camp on the site and use the falls as a natural shower to good effect. This is only one of the West Coast's many little known attractions, open only at present to those traveling by ship.

In the *Daily Colonist* on Saturday, March 16, 1946, James Mowat, Coalition member for Alberni, was reported to have spoken in the Legislature the previous day campaigning for road development to link the settlements along Vancouver Island's west coast. With the war over, the people of the coast were hoping that a start would be made that spring on a road to connect Tofino with Alberni. Mowat claimed that this road would help develop the island's tourist industry. He also supported Nancy Hodges in her pleas to aid people who were suffering from arthritis and other similar conditions. He told the House of "the curative qualities of the hot springs at Refuge Cove, long the mecca of rheumatism suffers among fishermen, miners and loggers on the West Coast."

Even after the long-awaited logging road to Port Alberni was completed in the summer of 1959, the first private vehicles wanting to get from Long Beach to Port Alberni could only use the logging road on the weekends when logging trucks were not active. It would remain a private industrial road until October 1964.

The Trail and the Hot Springs

Access to the actual hot springs changed over the years too. In the early years, it was a really good hike on a very primitive trail to get to the hot springs from the Clarke house. The same well-worn trail had been used since at least the 1700s. Over the years, Ivan and his family upgraded and straightened the original trail by cutting down smaller trees that were in the way, clearing the bush, levelling the ground and building boardwalks with approximately 40 stairs, all work done with hand tools.

Ten years after donating the park, Ivan was very concerned about the condition of the trail to the hot springs. The trail had fallen into disrepair due to the lack of maintenance by the Parks Ministry, who at the time brushed out the trail only once every year. Visitors to the park expressed their disappointment and began to complain about the condition of the trail. But it was the hot springs at the end of the trail that had always been the big attraction.

Ivan had hanging in his store for all to read, particularly the dubious, an analysis done by a Vancouver chemist. The water mainly contains sodium chloride (salt) along with calcium, iron oxides, sulphur and a few other chemical elements. The first study done on the content of the springs was in 1898, and another intensive study was written about by American-born geologist Charles Horace Clapp for the Canada Department of Mines Summary Report Geological Survey done in 1913.

Robert J. Phillip, who wrote his thesis on "Isotope Hydrogeology and Aqueous Geochemistry of Selected British Columbia Hot Springs" for the University of Ottawa, wrote: "In addition to being the only known substantial geothermal occurence on Vancouver Island, the Hotsprings Cove site is the oldest quantitatively-documented geothermal vent in Canada and has exhibited remarkable geochemical stability over the past century."

Nicholson wrote that many long-time west coast residents believed the water was the "Elixir of Life," or fountain of youth. In years gone by, people used the pools for relief from many ailments, particularly those of a rheumatic type, and some drank the water for medicinal purposes or did their laundry in it. They are naturally occurring, enclosed in the bedrock, and are like luxury baths, but not quite as comfortable, and the uneven rocky surface that they are nestled in can be hard to clamber over. The downside of doing laundry in the water, before that practice was banned, is that clothing smelled like sulphur when it was dry—not a problem for those who did not mind going around smelling like a box of wooden matches.

Nicholson wrote of an old prospector who lived to be 90 who made an annual pilgrimage to the hot springs, crediting his longevity to the curative properties of the water. He rowed the 40 miles (64 km) in his rowboat and camped beside the spring. He bathed in them several times a day and drank as much of the water as he could, then rowed back home, looking and feeling like a new person. He also told of a gentleman from Tacoma, crippled with arthritis, who visited on his yacht for 20 years to soak in the springs, as well as a doctor from Portland, Oregon, who came in by plane.

For years, hot springs in general were thought to have curative properties for numerous aliments, which would naturally attract a wide range of people to them. As far back as 1887, Harrison Hot Springs near Agassiz, BC, advertised in the *Daily Colonist* that the medical profession "strongly recommended" their hot springs for the cure of "dropsy [a collection of water in the body], gravel [kidney stones], rheumatism, neuralgia [pain in a sensory nerve], paralysis, sciatica, dyspepsia [heartburn], salt rheum, eczema, mercurial poisoning, venereal diseases, dipsomania, nervous and kidney complaints, malaria, fever and ague."

"Ladies will derive great benefit from a course of the bath for all complaints, while they [the hot springs] are excellent for the complexion," the advertising proclaimed. "No better tonic to restore tired nature exists."

Victoria newspapers had long run ads for businesses that were touting their products as being just as good as the medicinal values of hot springs. Going back to 1897, Hudson Medical Institute, with offices in Stockton and San Francisco, was advertising in the Victoria newspapers that:

Hudyan is purely vegetable. Strengthens and invigorates and tones the entire system. It is as cheap as any other remedy.

HUDYAN cures debility, nervousness, emissions and develops and restores weak organs. Pains in the backs, losses by day or night stopped quickly. Over 2000 private endorsements.

Send for circular and testimonials.

TAINTED BLOOD—Impure blood due to serious private disorders, carries myriads of sore-producing germs. "Then comes sore throat, pimples, copper-coloured spots, ulcers in the mouth, old sores and falling hair. You can save a trip to Hot Springs by writing for "Blood Book" to the old physicians at the Hudson Medical Institute."

For all the years that Ivan lived at the cove, he never looked his age and he credited his youthful looks to the hot springs, his personal fountain of youth. The truth be told, his mother looked amazingly youthful, even after giving birth to 12 children, so he just had good family genes for his youthful looks. The Clarke family would go at least every Sunday to take a bath in the hot springs. Sometimes they would take along some eggs to boil in the hot water while they were there. They carefully placed these around the 6-inch (15-cm) fissure where the water erupted up through the ground. They had to be very fast retrieving the eggs when they were ready so as not to scald their hands.

Ivan's wooden bathtub at the springs (see chapter 9) came with posted rules: "Please drain the tub after use, rinse out and then refill until the water over flows." The next person who came along simply had to swing the fill pipe back above the tub and let the hot water blend with the water that had already cooled off, until it was the perfect temperature. The water is soft, so any brand of bar soap lathered up nicely in the water. Depending how hot the water was, about 15 to 20 minutes was as long as one could last submerged in the tub. Later on, even when they had a proper bathtub in their house, the Clarke children still walked out to the hot springs to bathe.

When they returned from the springs they often brought their dad back a gallon jar of the spring water, which Ivan would drink. He used it for his own medicinal purposes. Hugh said he also used to drink the spring water when it was cold, and it tasted good!

When the *Maquinna* passengers were finally able to go ashore at Hot Springs Cove, they also used to bottle the water for the health-giving qualities allegedly contained in it.

Probably because Ivan did not have the water licence to the hot springs, he did not try bottling and selling the spring water. There had been the ads in the Victoria newspapers going back to 1893 for "Thorpe and Co.'s sole agent for St. Alice Mineral Water, from the Celebrated Harrison Hot Springs, A Mild Aperient and Great Aid to Digestion. Sold by all Grocers and Druggists. Factories, Victoria and Vancouver, B.C." And there was the mineral water from Banff Springs, which starting in 1910 was bottled and advertised as "Natural Mineral Water, tonic and invigorating."

People from the Nuu-chah-nulth First Nations had of course discovered and made use of the hot springs since time immemorial.

The waterfall at the hot springs is about the temperature of a very hot shower, which was too hot for most visitors even if they tried to slowly ease under it. The first pool seats three or four and is like a very hot bath (around

Until the mid-'80s, visitors to the hot springs could soak in a clawfoot bathtub requisitioned by the Clarke boys from neighbouring Estevan Point. Their nephew Robert Foster tested the water's temperature during a visit in the decade before the Parks Department removed the tub. Foster Family Collection

120F/50C) that one has to get into very gingerly. There are five lower inter-connected pools, each fed by the other, each just a bit cooler than the previous one as the water gets closer to the ocean.

On the "never-payment plan," the Clarke boys disconnected and helped themselves to a claw-foot bathtub from an old building at Estevan Point, loaded it in their boat and brought it ashore just below the hot springs. They manhandled the tub up and nestled it in the rocks on the north side of the springs, a little bit farther down than the wooden bathtub was, but still above the falls. The tub could be filled by a hose fed from the steaming creek. Once filled, it still took about a half an hour for the water to cool down to a bearable temperature. The Parks Department had it removed around the mid-'80s.

A very large number of fishermen used to bathe in the pools every year, many in their "birthday suits," but that changed once women settled in the cove and started to visit the hot springs, along with the women and girls from the fishboats, yachts and cabin cruisers! The fishermen would spend hours bathing in the hot springs, washing off the dirt, grime, and the smell of diesel fuel before relaxing in pools of varying temperatures. Twenty minutes, three-quarters submerged in water in the middle pool, was more than enough for me to start to feel uncomfortable, as well as thirsty.

1950s and '60s at the Cove

In the early 1950s, the Clarke family built a new four-bedroom house attached to the north side of the store. They used recycled materials off the stranded bunkhouse barge, so the house ended up with many of the bunkhouse features. They recycled the studs, joists and rafters as well as doors and windows. Ivan, the boys and Fred Thornberg all helped build it. Patsy and Diane shared a bedroom. Hugh, Billy and Jimmy shared a room, and Art and Buddy were in another. Ivan and Mabel had their room off the kitchen.

Nada described the layout of the old house, the new house and the store, referring to a picture of her father standing on the boardwalk just outside the store (next page). In the picture the house is in the back, and the side window that can be seen was a bedroom, looking out on a small square garden that her father was standing in front of. They could walk past the end of the building and go into the oil shed and the water well. The water storage tank can be

In the early 1950s, the Clarkes moved out of their original home, the shingled building behind Ivan, into a new four-bedroom home that he built using materials from the stranded bunkhouse. The general store is to the left, and a garden to the right. Foster Family Collection

seen in the top right of the picture. The walk at the back of the house went across the creek to the teacher's house, schoolhouse and former restaurant.

The next addition was also built from the recycled materials salvaged from the stranded barge. That addition went on in a line from the old bedrooms, kitchen and porch, and had two bedrooms on the end near the creek, one in front and the other on the back. There was a small bedroom next to the back one, with the bathroom next to it. The front room was in front of all of this, then came the kitchen with a window looking out back. It had kitchen counters with an oil stove that was directly across from the dining table, which had bench seats. There was a front window. The area behind the kitchen wall, across from the stove, was another bedroom with a door off the kitchen. The water tank was in behind the stove chimney and the back wall was used to hang coats and other things. The door out to the laundry room had a bathroom off it, which was all part of the old house.

The outdoors were accessed through an inside door into what was the old kitchen, but was then used as a packing and storage room for the store. The old main bedroom, with a window looking out over a small garden, was used for storing extra boxes. There was a doorway into the front of the new store at the top of the outside stairs, which was where the post office was situated. Another door with locks on it was off the old kitchen and small hallway into the store.

The store counter started near that door, went down the side and turned and went across the front. This is where the fish tallies were done. On the front and the side were groceries with the old cash register by the small window. A long porch or veranda was also added across the front of the new house so that all the rooms at the front now looked into the porch.

Nada nostalgically went on to say "sitting at my table now, I can still picture the boys saying a boat is coming, then the name of the boat, and I've got to go and buy fish."

At the end of June 1957, Mabel headed down to Victoria to attend the funeral of her father, who had passed away in St. Joseph's Hospital, and to spend some time with her mother and brother.

In 1958, there were about 20 Indigenous families living at the cove, and about 20 other people. Before the Catholic church was built at the head of the cove, the priest who visited three or four times a year would sleep in the top bunk above Hugh, after spending Sunday afternoon and evening drinking with Ivan. In the 1950s and '60s, Les Talbot lived in one of Ivan's cabins at the cove. He was a former Port Alberni bank manager who changed careers and became a prospector and fisherman. He helped watch over the store whenever needed. Ivan also rented out a cabin to George Rae-Arthur and his family until George bought a lot of his own across the cove. Times were good for Ivan—in 1960 he had a reported income from the federal government of $11,805, and a year later it had grown to $18,222.

Fred Thornberg, who sometimes worked in Ivan's fish camp, also lived in a cabin on Ivan's property on the north side of "God's Pocket," just up past Ralph's cabin. His brother, Andreas, had property of his own on the other side of the cove. Their father was part of Justice Louis A. Audette's Sealing Commission Hearing in the summer of 1914 and told how he had to close down his general store at Ahousat when the Indigenous people stopped pelagic sealing in 1911. Fred and Andreas both put in claims of close to $8,000 each for the loss of their livelihoods as steersmen to the Royal Commission established by the Canadian government, but received only about $200 each in compensation.

Ivan arrived in Refuge Cove 22 years after the North Pacific Seal Convention was signed on July 7, 1911, halting commercial pelagic sealing.

By pure coincidence, Frederick Elworthy, the father of Ivan's former brother-in-law, Harold Elworthy, was the secretary for the Board of Trade in Victoria for 40 years. The Board of Trade was very involved with the pelagic sealing industry out of Victoria. Frederick would have known of many Ahousaht former seal hunters like Fred and Andreas Thornberg, as well as their father. The Ahousaht seal hunters were the ones most sought after by the captains of the sealing schooner fleet based out of Victoria. Frederick would also have known of Ivan's brother-in-law, Captain Jim Olson, from his sealing days.

On June 10, 1961, a brand new west coast passenger and freight service was inaugurated by Barkley Sound Transportation Ltd. Captain Eason Young, president of the firm, announced that the 129-foot *Uchuck III* was going to be used for this service. It left Port Alberni early Saturday morning and Hot Springs Cove was among the ship's many new stops.

In 1961 Ivan and Mabel's eldest daughter, Nada, married Robert (Bob) Foster of Port Alberni at Centennial United Church on Gorge Road in Victoria. Bob met Nada in Hot Springs Cove while he was fishing on his boat, *Bunyit*. Later he purchased the 1946 35-foot double-ender (canoe stern) troller, *Evian*, and then the 36-foot, 2-inch *Pacific Sunset*.

On June 13, 1962, William (Billy) Clarke accidently died of carbon monoxide poisoning on his fishing skiff while docked at Hot Springs Cove. Funeral arrangements were made through Stevens Funeral Home in Port Alberni and he was buried three days later in Tofino's Seaview Cemetery. Not long afterwards, my mother received a letter in the mail from the family lawyer asking if she wanted to be an executrix for his estate, as Billy did not have a will. She declined the offer and left the job to her other siblings.

In early September 1962, the Rev. Father Thomas Lobsinger, the flying priest of the west coast of Vancouver Island who covered the Oblate missions of Opitsat, Hot Springs Cove and Ahousat, announced he was leaving for a new job in Williams Lake around Christmas. He would stay at Ivan's while he was at the cove. His replacement had not been announced at the time. Up until a few years earlier he would travel to his missions by boat, but in 1960 a float plane had been donated to the mission district by an American who used to have property on Centre Island in Esperanza Inlet.

It was also in 1962 that George Nicholson's book *Vancouver Island's West Coast 1762–1962* was published. Nicholson had for many years submitted articles to the "Islander" section of the Sunday *Daily Colonist* about the history of the west coast of Vancouver Island, which included many articles about Ivan and the cove, and finally he had compiled enough stories to write the book. After his finished manuscript was declined by the well-known publishers of the day, Nicholson decided to self-publish it, which at that time was basically unheard of.

Ivan knew about the book and Nicholson's publishing issues and decided to more than generously help his friend Nicholson finance the costs of printing his book. Ivan was interested in the history of the coast also, and it didn't hurt that Nicholson had given Ivan much more than a passing mention in the book. In 1962, Nicholson had his hardcover book printed at Morriss Printing in Victoria.

Vancouver Island's West Coast 1762–1962 became an enormous success, being reprinted at least a dozen times. Selling in excess of 10,000 copies mainly in BC, it became the go-to reference book at the time for the history of the west coast of Vancouver Island. In later life, Nicholson mentioned to his grandson Colin many times how much he was indebted to Ivan for his generosity. This explains why, when my mother let me take her copy of the book to school for an elementary school project and it did not return home with me, she was none too pleased.

In late February 1963, Mabel left Ivan and her family at the cove and headed back down to Victoria to spend time with her brother Patrick, who was not well. He passed away in the middle of March. He was the only uncle that the Clarke children really got to know when he was living up at the cove, besides their uncle Ralph.

Tidal Wave:
Hot Springs Cove Hit Hard

O n Good Friday 1964 at 5:26 p.m., an earthquake of magnitude 9.2 occurred in the Prince William Sound region of Alaska. This caused the seafloor in the sound to lift, and the tectonic movements in the Gulf of Alaska created a huge tsunami that hit the west coast of British Columbia and the United States in the darkness of night.

Except for the Gulf of Alaska, the BC coastline suffered the greatest damage of any in the Pacific area. Outside Alaska, the two places most heavily damaged were Port Alberni and Crescent City, California.

At 11 p.m., as usual, the generator that supplied electricity to the entire Hot Springs Nuu-chah-nulth village at the north end of the cove was shut off. With no tsunami warning systems in place, and with the long-distance phone lines having closed down at nine p.m. as usual, Hot Springs Cove residents were completely unprepared for the flood of water that arose rapidly from the ocean. They had no idea what was going on, only that they needed to make it to higher ground before their homes were lifted away with them still in it. In the darkness of night, as they scrambled to higher ground, entire houses were swept away by the water. A few of those houses were actually on Ivan's property, Lot 1371. Only two of the eighteen comparatively new Indigenous homes survived the March 27 disaster. The new Roman Catholic Church of the Immaculate Conception and light plant building were also destroyed. It was reported that, in proportion to its population, the Hot Springs Cove Indigenous village received greater damage than any other place on the British Columbia coast. On August 9, 1964, the *Daily Colonist* recounted the events of that evening.

> The Indian village is (or was) situated at the head of the bay, hence it received the full force of the three successive tidal surges. Fortunately, there were no causalities, but only because the first wave came in gradually and gave the occupants of the houses, when they found water over the floor, time to seek the safety of the higher ground. It was the second wave that caused the greatest damage. Most families lost all their personal belongings.
>
> Between waves, menfolk lucky enough to find their canoes, some of which were washed to sea, managed to reach their fishboats anchored in the bay.

On Good Friday 1964, a 9.2-magnitude earthquake off the southern coast of Alaska unleashed a series of tsunami waves in Hot Springs Cove. Sixteen of the eighteen Hesquiaht First Nation homes in the cove were lost, including the Amos family home, photographed floating by Ivan's wharf the next day. Major George Nicholson Collection/Ken Gibson Collection

Ivan's steamer wharf and its approaches were extensively damaged. According to Tofino historian Ken Gibson, "It's a miracle that the whole wharf never floated away." The water had risen above the top of the vertical log pilings that Ivan's wharf was built around and it could have easily floated away. The fuel depot was also damaged and the fuel lines leading from the tanks on the slope behind the store were broken, which caused fuel to be spilled into the cove. Fortunately there were three inline safety valves for each tank, which the fuel had to flow through, and the first ones that Ivan and his boys managed to get to were turned off to prevent his fuel tanks from completely emptying into the cove. Several of Ivan's other shore installations were also badly damaged.

As the *Daily Colonist* noted at the time, only Mother Nature knows why the damage at the small Nuu-chah-nulth village almost opposite Ivan's operation was negligible.

People responded quickly. The day after the tsunami, the St. Vincent de Paul Society sent three tons of clothing to be delivered to the approximately 70 people who had lost all their possessions at Hot Springs Cove. The clothing would be transported to Tofino first before making its way to the cove.

Ivan's wharf was littered with debris the morning after the earthquake. Despite tsunami waves well above the vertical pilings, the wharf surprisingly did not float away. Major George Nicholson Collection/Ken Gibson Collection

On April 11, Ivan phoned Mayor Les Hammer of Port Alberni to request carpenters and labourers to help rehabilitate the village of Hot Springs Cove, which had been severely damaged after the tsunami. But such help was, of course, already in short supply after the damage that Port Alberni had also received.

The Mennonite organization of BC was dispatched from Vancouver after hearing of their plight, offering the services of many of their skilled labourers and technicians. The organization had already been planning to send electricians to the cove to reinstall their electrical plant, which had been sent to Vancouver for repairs prior to the tsunami. Meanwhile, residents of the cove's village were trying to make the remaining homes habitable for their families before fishing season officially opened on April 15. Indian Affairs branch engineers were already at the cove and had already been informed of the help coming their way. The Canadian Coast Guard also mobilized their skin diving crew to help retrieve possessions such as kitchen stoves and other household items that had sunk into the sea.

On April 14, the *Colonist* reported that United Church minister Rev. William Robinson, on behalf of the village members, wanted to express his thanks to the organizations, churches and individuals who had donated truckloads of clothing and supplies. They had been overwhelmed at the response. Many of the village members ultimately ended up having more than they ever had before the tsunami. A couple days later, the *Colonist* reported that the fishermen were ready to move back into their homes at the head of Hot Springs Cove, and that they were on track for the fishing season. They were living in temporary accommodations until after the fishing season. Sometime later, the government rebuilt the village on higher ground and eventually about 10 families moved back into it.

Insurance adjusters at the time estimated the damage along the British Columbia coast would total $2.5–3 million. The final damage estimate was more than $10 million, with $64,750 of that total coming from Hot Springs Cove.

Gold Medal Surfaces

Many years ago I was pleasantly surprised to find out that in the aftermath of the tsunami a member of my Clarke family had been able to play a role in proving that an injustice had been done to the Hesquiaht people many years before.

I have been an avid reader of the history of British Columbia and its people since 1975. As a result, I have read many accounts of an ugly blemish in British Columbian history, when James Douglas, the governor of the Colony of British Columbia, sent orders to Captain Henry Mist to take the 180-foot 6-inch British Gun Vessel HMS *Sparrowhawk* up the coast as a show of force to find out who was responsible for the alleged murders of the survivors of the 456-ton ship *John Bright*, which had run aground on Estevan Point in 1869.

That year, Hesquiaht chief John Anayitzachist was one of two people hanged on the beach in front of their own people as a lesson to them for his supposedly having murdered the *John Bright* survivors. Five years later, in 1874, the gibbet on which they were hanged still stood as a solemn reminder.

On October 10, 1882, the *New York Times* ran an article about the American barque *Malleville*, which was shipwrecked near Hesquiat with no survivors. John Anayitzachist's son, Aime Anutspator, now the Hesquiaht chief, carried on the tradition of retrieving the bodies and burying them. For his services, US president Chester Arthur awarded him with $200 and a gold medal, on which the inscription read: "The President of the United States of America—to Aime Anutspator, Chief of the Hesquiaht Tribe, British Columbia, for his humane services to the crew of the wrecked American ship Malleville."

In 2010, the newspaper *Ha-Shilth-Sa* (Canada's oldest Indigenous newspaper, out of Port Alberni) reported that Ivan's son Art Clarke had contacted the Amos family, descendants of John Anayitzachist through his son Aime Anutspator, whose home had first washed down the cove as far as Ivan's dock in the 1964 tsunami. Art handed them an old envelope on which the words, "March 2?/64 Might belonge [sic] to Alex Amos of Hot Springs Cove" were written. In the envelope was the gold medal that had been thought long lost by the Amos family, which Art had found in the wreckage of the Amos house after it had washed ashore near Sharp Point.

The Amos family did not get an apology from the provincial government, but in November 2012, the descendants of Anayitzachist, having used the medal as evidence that their ancestor did not murder the survivors of the *John Bright*, took part in a reconciliation feast with Ida Chong,

BC's minister of Aboriginal relations and reconciliation, to close the door on this past hurt.

"The Province expresses its sincere regret and laments that Hesquiaht members, and family in particular, were forced to bear witness to such violence and for the trauma and pain they have endured," Chong said. "It is our hope that from this time forward the relationship between BC and the Hesquiaht people is strengthened and flourishes."

Changes in the Clarke Family

In the same year as the tsunami, and just over two years after Billy's death, Mabel Clarke passed away of a heart attack on July 6, 1964, at 60 years of age, at home in Hot Springs Cove, leaving Ivan with seven children from their marriage. Her body was transported to Tofino, and Corporal I. R. Smith with the Tofino RCMP detachment filled out the death registration for the family. Ivan picked out the top-of-the-line casket for Mabel through Thomas Gibson, who was the undertaker in Tofino at the time.

In the Port Alberni newspaper on July 7, it was reported that Mrs. Mabel Clarke, wife of Ivan Clarke and leading citizen of Hot Springs Cove, had passed away on Monday. The newspaper went on to mention Ivan Clarke's various roles in the community before noting that, besides her husband and seven children, Mrs. Clarke's survivors included her mother in Victoria.

Funeral services were held in St. Columba's Anglican Church in Tofino on July 8 and she was buried in Tofino's Seaview Cemetery next to her son Billy.

On the same day as Mabel's death, the *Colonist* reported that the army naval training yacht HMCS *Oriole* left Victoria for a training cruise around the island and that one of their many stops was Hot Springs Cove. The cove had also been one of many ports of call for another kind of vessel, the 51-foot 8-inch *Blue Fjord*, not too long after the tsunami. The *Blue Fjord* had left Victoria on May 17, 1964, on a round-the-island tour to allow travelling salesmen to personally meet some of their customers, but several vacationers also filled the passenger list that first year and had an enjoyable time.

On August 17, it was announced that a contract had been awarded for a float construction job at Hot Springs Cove, with Thomas Gibson and Sons' tender being accepted, at a price of $10,000. The float, which was to be started in September, was going to measure 80 by 36 feet (24×11 m). Included in the tender was the removal of an old freight shed.

A month later, on September 16, Ivan was appointed an enumerator for Hot Springs Cove. But even though he was so well settled in at the cove, Ivan's pioneer spirit hadn't died. In 1965 he was having a conversation with his long-time friend J. Alex McKenzie, talking about the great fish-producing rivers in the Alaska Panhandle. Ivan's eyes lit up and he said, "I'd love to tackle a deal like that."

Ivan and Mabel's second daughter, Patricia (Patsy), had married Peter Moseley in the lounge of Centennial United Church, in Victoria, in early October, with Ivan giving his daughter in marriage. After raising their family, Patsy spent a lot of time on the water with Peter, fishing on their 1950 41-foot 7-inch troller *Blaze*.

In the middle of December 1964, the Clarke family suffered another loss when Mabel's mother passed away in the Richmond Heights Private Hospital in Victoria, only three weeks after being admitted. Nada, who was married and had trained as a nurse, lived in Victoria with her small family. She took care of the details for the family.

Two and a half years later, in December 1968, Thomas Gibson and Sons was awarded another float contract for the federal government at Hot Springs Cove. They were to build five 80-foot (24-m) floats, which were going to be moored with 10 cement anchors, with the work expected to be completed before the new year.

A second project at the cove was the removal of the superstructure of the present government wharf at a cost of $10,000.

Family Business:
Ivan's Children Learn the Ropes

Hugh Clarke did not hear about the tsunami damage at Hot Springs Cove until after the disaster because by then he was living at Ahousat, which, due to its location, did not receive any damage. Ivan had helped arrange the purchase for Hugh of the store, all the outbuildings and 12 acres (4.8 hectares) of property in Ahousat for $25,000 in 1958, from his very good friend Gordon Gibson Sr., the lumber baron, also known as the "Bull of the Woods." This became a branch store of Ivan's at Hot Springs Cove and in 2019, Hugh still owns it.

One day in 1958, Hugh was returning to Hot Springs Cove in a friend's boat and was quite surprised to see his fishboat, *Start*, coming toward them. He had had it up for sale and it turned out his father had sold it, which gave Hugh the down payment to buy the Ahousat operation. However, he did borrow money from his father to purchase inventory for the store, which Patsy helped run.

Hugh and his siblings had learned a lot of their life skills from their father. Starting when they were young, Ivan taught his children how to splice ropes and tie knots, which he had learned during his tugboat days. These skills came in handy while living so close to the water. Ivan, having spent years working on the ocean, was the perfect person to teach his children all about reading the ocean, its tides, currents and hazards. He also taught them everything they needed to know about reading buoys, charts and marine flags, and how to run, navigate and maintain boats. Hugh was about eight years old when he borrowed a seine skiff from the Campbells to start fishing in Hot Springs Cove. He was ten when he started fishing outside the cove in a small boat that he had built, and he started commercial fishing, selling his fish to his father's fish camp at age twelve. He quit high school in Grade 9 and built a large boat shed and wooden boat ways on his father's property on the south side of the wharf. He also built a 25-foot (7.6-m) wood-fired steam box for bending wood, remnants of which can still be found in the nearby bush.

The following year, having never built one before, Hugh built a 32-foot double-ender (canoe stern) troller, which Ivan named *Start*. He searched the forests around Hot Springs Cove for just the right fir trees to cut down and

Like all of Ivan's children, Hugh learned how to work with his hands from an early age. He is pictured here in the double-ender troller Start *that he built while still a teenager.* Hugh S. Clarke Collection

shape to use for the 45 main mast and troller poles. When he was finished, Hugh used a come-a-long to winch *Start* down on the boat ways to the water.

If perchance a troller came in with a broken mast or troller pole, Hugh would send the owner into the forest at Hot Springs Cove and later on, on the mountain across from his operation at Matilda Creek, to cut down a fir or hemlock tree to shape into a new mast or pole for their boat. After Hugh finished building his boat, Ivan then had an open skiff built by the Ahousaht First Nation chief for Billy, who had started commercial fishing when he was 14. Not long after it was built, Hugh helped build a deck and cabin on Billy's boat.

Around 1950, Hugh built a small cottage on the south side of the start of the path to the hot springs. It still stands to this day in a clearing beside the boardwalk, although over the years it has been altered and expanded.

In about 1951, a call came in from a boat that was bringing Mabel home from the hospital in Tofino in the darkness. The water was rough and the boat was having trouble making any headway. Ivan went down and hired an 80-foot American Dragger that was moored to his dock to go out and rendezvous with the boat and bring Mabel back to the cove. But in the darkness,

Hugh's handiwork at Hot Springs Cove included this cottage, which stands to this day. The cove's ubiquitous boardwalks are visible in the lower right corner. Hugh S. Clarke Collection

the Americans were uncertain of the water and its dangers. Ivan, knowing how well he had taught Hugh, told the 15-year-old boy to go along and run the ship out and back. The Americans agreed and off they went, continually asking Hugh if he knew what he was doing and where he was going. After taking the boat through the narrows on the way down, they rendezvoused with the other boat not too far off the entrance to Matilda Inlet and safely brought Mabel home.

When Hugh came of age, Ivan took him to Victoria to get his driver's licence. After three lessons from the Garden City Driving School instructor, priced at three dollars per lesson, Hugh was told he was ready to take his test. Students were permitted to take two lessons per day, so Hugh decided to take five more lessons in three days before taking his test, just so he could see more of Victoria. Finally, he went to the motel near the motor vehicle office on Menzies Street where his father was staying to get him to sign the papers for the licence. Ivan had consumed too much alcohol, so didn't cooperate, and Hugh lost his chance to get his licence. He never bothered to try again, so to this day he has never had one. However, he did drive to Port Alberni and back to Tofino many times in his younger days.

The sale of Start *provided the down payment for Hugh to purchase the old Gibson Brothers operation at Ahousat, pictured here in the late 1930s. The original general store is in the centre. Hugh expanded the operation over the years, adding a restaurant, family home, motel, fish camp and boat ways.* Hugh S. Clarke Collection

Ivan was very good friends with the officers in the local RCMP detachment and spent a lot of time drinking with them. As Hugh was so knowledgeable about boating, the area and the waters on the west coast of Vancouver Island, the RCMP were very interested in having him join the detachment to become their boat operator for that area. Ivan took Hugh down to Victoria to sign up, but in the end Hugh wanted no part of it.

Hugh fished commercially in a troller for almost two years and by the later 1950s, had settled down and was operating a Canadian Fishing Company camp that he had brought into Ahousat on a scow. At first the scow had been moored down by the village, but later on it was towed up the inlet to Matilda Creek. The scow had a store, marine fuel station, ice house and living accommodations on it. The small Ahousat General Store owned by the Gibson brothers had been shut down, except for the post office, which was being run by watchman and acting postmaster Bert L. Clayton in the interim.

Not long after his purchase of the Ahousat operation, Hugh moved the post office down to the barge, and was sworn in as acting postmaster on April 1, 1963.

Ahousat is at latitude 49°17' North and longitude 126°04' East on the southern end of Matilda Inlet. Interestingly, Hugh's property is at Matilda Creek, on the west side of Matilda Inlet, the very place where the *Maquinna* was tied up when Ivan had married Mabel 23 years earlier.

Developments

Hugh developed the Matilda Creek property over the years. At the time, watchman Bert Clayton was living in the original Gibson family house, and Hugh let him stay, as Bert's wife, Bunny, was not well. After she passed away in October 1964, Hugh moved into the main house himself.

Over the years, with the help of some locals and his brother Raymond, Hugh expanded the store, eventually adding a restaurant next to it. On the opposite side of the store he built a new house for his family. All along the front of the store Hugh placed blasted rock up to 18 feet (5.5 m) deep in spots, replacing the old boardwalk. He was taught how to blast by some old prospectors. Today, the original Gibson family house is leased by the University of Victoria Whale Research Lab.

More or less mirroring his father's business at Hot Springs, Hugh also had a fish-buying camp, general store, marine fuel depot, post office, motel, restaurant and boat ways, which he built using metal rails that had been bought for one at Hot Springs, but had never been installed. He has hauled boats as long as 65 feet (19.7 m) up onto the ways, but prefers to stick to a maximum of 50 feet (15 m). Today, he will still bring boats up out of the water on his ways for a very reasonable charge. At present, the next closest boat ways are at Ucluelet.

Hugh installed boat ways at Ahousat from rails originally purchased for a boat ways at Hot Springs Cove. Diane Kaehn photo

Hugh estimates that over the years he has replaced over 100 boat engines at his place.

Hugh first met his future wife, Margaret (Maggie) Campbell, at the cove after Ivan had hired her sister to help Mabel with the younger children. Maggie went to Vancouver for nurses' training. When she eventually started working at the Tofino General Hospital, Hugh thought he had better make his move, so he would get into his boat at midnight and head down to Tofino to see her after her shift, and then return to Ahousat in the wee hours of the morning. He married Maggie in Ahousat in 1963.

Hanging from a beam in Hugh's store is a small wooden contraption that he enjoys puzzling visitors with. When they ask what the heck it is, after allowing for some guessing, he pulls it down and shows off the 65-year-old wooden and metal automatic boat bilge pump that he invented as a teenager, before there was even such a thing.

These days Hugh has to pre-order his fuel, which arrives about once a month. He has to pay for the barge to bring the tanker truck in on, as well as the truck time itself, but he still sells his fuel for less than the price in Tofino. He has three tanks, holding about 50,000 litres (11,000 gallons) each, two for diesel and one for marine gas. He has a smaller tank for stove oil. Boats from all around come day and night to his fuel depot, from opening to closing time, which is at about nine p.m., but he'll stay open later during the summer, or if it happens to be busy. He's not selling as much fuel as he used to, now that the fishery seems to have moved north. When his store sign says he does not open until nine in the morning, he means it. Incoming boats, for the most part, radio ahead to let Hugh know they are coming in for fuel.

Hugh owned a concrete truck or two that he barged around along with a loader, navvy jack and other equipment to any job sites that needed concrete. And along the way, if he needed a board cut, he also had his own sawmill. He ran all of this by himself in the beginning, with the help of Patsy, until she got married and settled down in Victoria. In about 1983, Patsy returned to Ahousat during the busy season to cook in the restaurant, and did so up until several years ago.

On June 10, 1963, Hugh took the postmaster's oath and was sworn in as the Ahousat postmaster by Les Hammer, who at that time was an alderman in Port Alberni. Les was also the postal inspector, making trips out to all the remote post offices.

After the *Maquinna* stopped servicing the coast, a North Arm Transport freight boat from Vancouver would bring supplies and mail to Hugh and Ivan's stores twice a week; later on they were serviced by Ahousaht Freight Service.

Toward the end of April 1967, after fielding many complaints about their service, the federal Post Office Department announced that under their new schedule all mail would be transported by plane, rather than by boat, from many west coast offices, including Ahousat and Hot Springs Cove.

In late June 1967, the planes and operation formerly controlled by BC Airlines in the Albernis received approval for transfer of ownership to three partners—Mike Carr-Harris, Bill McCulty and pilot Bob Vickers. One day a young woman and a small girl entered their Ocean Air Limited office with an armful of items, including a small chainsaw and several empty gas cans. "Can you drop these off at Hot Springs Cove?" she asked while going back for a second load. It was just another busy day at their Port Alberni float base. In 2002, Hugh received a recognition letter from the Canadian Postmasters and Assistants Association for his 39-year membership (at that time). In 2004, his daughter, Iris Huebner, started working in the Tofino post office, and in 2009 she became its postmaster, thus becoming the third generation in the family to run a post office. Until very recently, Hugh held the postmaster position, sorting the mail when it came in, except for some time a few years ago while he was recovering from a stroke. Iris ran the Ahousat post office while her father was convalescing and visited twice a week to help sort mail for him. In May 2017, Hugh's granddaughter Shelby became the postmaster at Ahousat, making her the fourth-generation postmaster in the family.

Other Interests

After he settled in Ahousat, Hugh also took line repair calls for BC Telephone Company, as his boat was faster than BC Tel company lineman George Rae-Arthur's and he could get to the problem lines more quickly. He still has, hanging on the wall, the store's original crank telephone, which was used until the 1960s when there was still a BC Telephone operator in the Ahousat village. The store ring was one long and three short. With modern technology and the use of satellites, the original lines and poles are now long gone—although cellphone service leaves a lot to be desired. Hugh says that if you

Technological change was slow to come to Ahousat. This crank telephone was used in Hugh's store into the 1960s and remains on display to this day. Cellphone service continues to be limited. Diane Kaehn photo

stand at the far end of the motel on the second-floor balcony and hold your phone just right, you sometimes might get reception. I've only managed to get one short text out in the middle of the night during my visits.

Hugh used his own speedboat for what was the very first water taxi service to Tofino from Ahousat. He charged $15 a boatload one way. Today there are many water taxis running back and forth all day and night and it now costs $20 per person one way, which is still a good deal. When his children were in elementary school, Hugh would take them down to the village in his boat, and when they went to high school the boat was used to take them down to Tofino on Sunday night and bring them home on Friday afternoon.

One night, years ago, when Hugh had been drinking with his brother-in-law Bob Foster they heard a heck of a racket outside the back door of the original family house. With a belly full of whiskey and his rifle in hand, Hugh headed for the door with Bob right behind him. Just outside the door was a cougar with its jaws around the throat of one of Hugh's goats. It was so close, he could have grabbed the cougar by the tail. With Bob proclaiming, "You'll never hit it," and at the same time helping to steady him, Hugh shot the cougar in the head. The head of that cougar is still proudly mounted in his store.

From 1979 to 2013, Hugh owned the 26-foot tug *Majugin*, built in 1949, and at one time owned up to four trollers, which he would lease out, complete with a fishing licence. Today he owns the 1967 29-foot fibreglass Deltaga troller *Sonya*, which was up for sale at the time of writing. As well, he owns the 1968 36-foot freight boat *New Whitecliff*, which is run by his son, Keith, to bring in supplies for the store. It also services the Ahousat village down the inlet. Many people called Hugh their "Unk," a term of fondness used by his relatives in the village. Hugh, who is known to everyone else as Hughie, has owned the Ahousat operation for almost 60 years.

Ivan had his fish-buying barge at the end of the wharf at Hot Springs Cove, and Hugh also had one at the Ahousat wharf to ice and store the fish

Like his father before him, Hugh Clarke dedicated his life to providing a multitude of services for a small community on the west coast of Vancouver Island. He has owned his Ahousat operation, photographed in 2015, for almost sixty years. Diane Kaehn photo

that they bought. Fish would be shipped out on a packer twice a week—more often if necessary during the busy season, and only once a week or less when it was not so busy. When it was getting too expensive for Canadian Fishing Company to run its packers down the coast to Victoria, the fish were trucked out of Tofino.

Incorporation

On June 30, 1966, Ivan H. Clarke and Sons Ltd. became incorporated, with Ivan becoming executive director, as well as the president and a shareholder. Hugh also became an executive director and shareholder. For the start-up, there were ten common shares with a value of one dollar each. Two of Ivan's lawyer's secretaries were given one common share each, probably for paperwork reasons, as later in October one was transferred into Ivan's name, giving him nine common shares, and the other into Hugh's name, giving him one common share. All of the Ivan H. Clarke and Sons Hot Springs Cove property, buildings, installations and holdings became part of this company. When Ivan passed away, his nine common shares had risen in value to $22,792.95.

The company was established with two objectives.

(a) To import, export, buy, sell and deal in goods, wares and merchandise of all kinds or descriptions, and to carry on any or all lines of business as a manufacturers, producers, processors, merchants, distributors, commission agents and wholesale and retail importers and exporters; and, without in anywise limiting the generality of the foregoing, to acquire, construct and operate warehouses, stores and shops.

(b) To acquire, own and carry on the business of wholesale and retail dealers in and purchasers and manufacturers of groceries and all kinds and classes of goods, wares and merchandise connected therewith and to act as agents and to carry on all and any business, both wholesale and retail, as shopkeepers, and general merchants, manufacturers, shippers, general agents, exporters, importers, brokers and public warehousemen, and to buy, sell, make, manufacture, import and export, warehouse, store and deal in products of every description, goods, wares, merchandise or manufactured articles.

In about 1966, Ivan had his first heart attack. Heart-related issues, much too early in life, have claimed the lives of far too many of William and Annie Emma Clarke's descendants.

In 1967 or '68, Thomas Gibson and Sons were awarded the contract to install new floats and mooring facilities at the cove. That was about the same time that Ivan offered to sell the Hot Springs Cove business to Hugh for $65,000. In hindsight, Hugh wishes that he had taken up the offer, but he was still paying for his Ahousat operation.

Hot Springs Cove Store Closes

In 1968, economic reality eventually caused Ivan to close down his general store and his operation at Hot Springs Cove. With his family grown and out on their own, and Ivan not being able to afford to hire anybody, he found himself getting too old to run the place. Ivan first moved down to Surrey and then eventually retired to his hometown, Victoria.

The last list of inhabitants of Hot Springs Cove that I could find before Ivan closed down in 1968 was on the September 27, 1965, Canadian Government, Rural Preliminary List of Voters, for the Electoral District of Comox–Alberni, Rural Polling Division No. 33. The list of registered voters included 37 names.

Arthur Clarke

As with the rest of Ivan's sons, Arthur Clarke was adept at seafaring from a young age. At nine years old, Art improvised and made his first boat out of a fish box, corks firmly filling in the drain holes, and he used pieces of wood to paddle around the dock. In 1968, Art left Hot Springs Cove to work for Hugh at Ahousat. He bought the 1947 33-foot 7-inch troller *Gabriola Belle* and fished on it for two years. He then bought the troller *Joyce* and fished with it for six years. He really did not like rolling around out there. September to May, starting in 1970, he looked after the store, post office, marine fuel station and the Canadian Fishing Company fish camp at Hot Springs Cove until everything was closed down for good in 1973.

Art did not get married until he was in his mid-thirties. In 1974, he was on vacation in Hong Kong, visiting a church, when he met his future wife,

Art Clarke, shown in his home office in Tofino, worked for Hugh in Ahousat for a number of years before returning to oversee the final years of the Hot Springs Cove operation. He later ran a B&B and boat charters with his family in Tofino. Gloria Clarke Family Collection

Gloria. She was born in the Philippines and had been working in Hong Kong, sending money back home to her parents. For about half a year after returning home, Art wrote and courted Gloria through letters. She came to Canada in 1975 to marry the man who had been romancing her from Hot Springs Cove. After Art passed away, Gloria moved to Port Alberni.

From 1976 to 1979 Art worked for Canadian Fishing Company in Tofino. Robert M. "Pinky" Christensen and his wife, Marge, were also working for the company, where Pinky was doing the maintenance and Marge was the book-keeper/payroll clerk. When Tofino Packing became Tonquin Enterprises, they hired Pinky and Marge to manage their fish camp. The Christensens, in turn, hired Art to show them how to run the fish camp; he stayed there for two years.

A part-time job as Tofino harbour manager for small craft came up and Art got it, but he still worked part-time for the Christensens. He said it was a very good job, except when having to deal with drunk fishermen during herring season, but 2000 was his last year working, as his doctor said his heart was getting old. When he retired, Art and his family ran the Harbour Place B&B and Duffin Passage Charters on Main Street, which is now in the centre of Tofino. Like his father, Art also became a mason at Tofino-Manoah Lodge No. 141. Art passed away in 2012.

Ivan and Beatrice's first child, Beverley, married Barry Kaehn in 1951 in Cordova Bay, BC, and she trained to become a nurse. Beverley never did get

Beverley (Clarke) Kaehn never visited Hot Springs Cove in person, but she remained in contact with her father, Ivan. This photograph, circa 1970, is the only known picture of Beverley with her father after her parents divorced in 1933.

to see Hot Springs Cove, other than in pictures. As a teen, tired of living in an extended family household where everyone bossed her around, she wrote a letter asking her father if she could move up there. The idea was considered, but it was thought it would be best if she stayed with her mother. Even though Beverley did not live up there, and Ivan did not see her very often, he was very good to Beverley and her family over the years.

Ivan must have liked his name a lot because he used it in three of his children's names. Beverley, my mother, was never impressed with Ivanetta as her middle name! She passed away in 2008 in Victoria. Ivan's first name is not carried by any of his grandchildren or great-grandchildren, but his middle name Harrison is. Ivan and Beatrice's son Raymond, who was raised by his grandmother Clarke between Hot Springs Cove and later Victoria, became a well-known and respected carpenter in that city, where he married Pamela Paine in 1951. He passed away in 2007 in Victoria.

James (Jimmy) died on his 1967 40-foot 1-inch troller *Scania Queen* at Fisherman's Wharf in Victoria in 1977, leaving behind two children. Many of Ivan's grandchildren from his first and second marriages also became fishermen.

Ivan (Buddy) worked on fishboats and was working on a packer in 1978 when he died accidentally in Tofino.

In 1963, Ivan's daughter Diane graduated from the Molnar's School of Hairdressing, where she later became a teacher. She later went back to school to become a nurse and graduated in 1966. Although raised at Hot Springs Cove, she met her husband, Zenon Bainas, in Victoria, and they were married there in 1969. In 2011, Diane received the Lifetime Achievement Award from the Saskatchewan Association of Licensed Practical Nurses for providing exemplary service to the public over her entire nursing career. She passed away in Regina in 2013.

Of Ivan and Mabel's three remaining children, Hugh is still running his operation at Matilda Creek. Nada and her husband, Bob, retired in Victoria. After Bob retired they donated their troller *Evian* to the Tofino Botanical Gardens for tourists to enjoy. In 2014 after many years of enjoyment, the Botanical Gardens sent the *Evian* off in a traditional Viking ceremony. Bob passed away in early 2019. Patsy is retired and her husband, Peter, is still commercial fishing up the coast on their troller.

"True Grit" Pioneer Passes: *Ivan Remembered*

Ivan passed away November 12, 1971, in Victoria, a few years after his last year at Hot Springs Cove, and by 2019 he had approximately 100 descendants scattered throughout Canada and the United States. He was, in the words of Tofino historian Ken Gibson, a "true grit" pioneer whose story is the work he did to aid the new-found trolling industry in the years he spent at Hot Springs Cove.

Discussing Ivan's place in the history of Clayoquot Sound, Ken noted that in the mid-1890s, newly arrived Norwegians had started fishing in the area soon after they found that their Clayoquot Sound land pre-emptions were "barren." Keeping their land, the Norwegians fished for salmon, halibut and cod, using bait and nets. In the ten years prior to Ivan's arrival, the Japanese pioneered fishing with "lures, spoons, and wobblers." They had small, open, double-ended vessels and retreated to places of safety like Refuge Cove when the sea got angry.

Ivan inherited his pioneer spirit from his ancestors. He had no fear of getting far away from the big city and bright lights, to go partners with Mother Nature for a livelihood, to start all over again, against all odds, and he had the foresight for the business enterprise he eventually built at Hot Springs Cove, and to leave the lasting legacy that he did.

He really helped the fishing industry by leading by example, Ken said, suggesting to the big fish companies like BC Packers, Prince Rupert Co-op, Canadian Fishing Company and McCallums that they install buying stations (fish camps).

Hot Springs Cove was the last port heading north for any vessel until Nootka, and it was shoreward of the deep water. Ivan got in the fuel and supplies, and prepared everyone for what Ken called the "trek" around Estevan Point. Going around Estevan Point was "bloody awful in a seaway," Ken said. The word out there was always "give *Estevan* lots of room." The waves come down from northeast and up from southwest, causing a "confused sea" that tosses boats around. Also, Ken noted, it is "shallow for a long way." Hence the advice to go farther out. In fact, the shoals extend out some 2 miles (3 km), from 40 to 72 feet (12–22 m) deep, which is the cause of the rip tides in that area.

Ivan was a long-time member of the Tofino Chamber of Commerce, which Ken called "the voice of the people." Ivan supported navigation lights like the one on George Island, which is midway coming in from the sea past Hot Springs Cove on the north side of Flores Island. Ken said he also remembered Ivan campaigning every year for the annual improvement to the Hot Springs Trail, "never greatly, but firmly," and saw that when improvements were done the province got their "dollar value." Ivan also "never stopped reminding his local Member of Parliament in Ottawa and his local Member of the Legislative Assembly in Victoria what their job was."

In the *Daily Colonist* on October 19, 1955 Ivan took exception to a recent statement in Victoria by then-Transport Minister George Marler who said that a coast guard was unnecessary on the west coast was because "the present facilities appeared adequate, at least on paper." Tom Barnett, the Comox-Alberni M.P. speaking at a meeting in Cumberland, disagreed. He mentioned that the current BC coast air-sea rescue service was ill-equipped to handle any sort of emergency with their lack of high-speed vessels and badly needed to be supplemented.

Ivan was also of the opinion that a coast guard needed to be established. Although he praised the Tofino and Bamfield lifeboats for their services, he noted that they were "too small and their range too limited for aiding vessels in distress." Ivan's solution was to have two ships permanently serving the Island's west coast at two points, similar to the Pacific Salvage Company's

Ivan, shown shopping for a camera in 1970, left Hot Springs Cove in the late 1960s and spent the final years of his life in Victoria. He passed away there on November 12, 1971, one of the West Coast's last "true grit" pioneers.

salvage vessel the *Salvage King* that was currently serving the whole west coast of the island.

Ivan's death was announced in the *Daily Colonist* article dated November 16, 1971.

CLARKE—Suddenly in Victoria on November 13, Mr. Ivan H. Clarke, aged 68 years, of 3199 Balfour; a native son, well known fish-buyer, storekeeper and Standard Oil agent at Hot Springs Cove, V.I., for 33 years. He leaves ... five sons, Raymond Clarke of Victoria; Hugh, Arthur, Jim and Ivan all of Ahousat, V.I.; four daughters, Mrs. B.H. (Beverley) Kaehn, Mrs. R. (Nada) Foster, Mrs. Diane Bainas and Mrs. Patsy Moseley, all of Victoria, 21 grandchildren; three brothers,

Ralph and Hugh in Victoria and Albert in Vancouver; one sister, Mrs. Elsie Kinnear of Victoria. He was a member of the Victoria–Columbia Lodge No. 1, A.F. and A.M. Victoria.

Funeral service in McCall Bros Chapel.

A month following his death, on December 12, the family posted the following in the newspaper under "Cards of Thanks".

We wish to express our heartfelt thanks and appreciation to our relatives, friends and neighbours for cards of sympathy, letters and messages during our recent sad bereavement. Special thanks to Rev. Percy Wills. –

The sons and daughters of Ivan H. Clarke

The first time I can remember my parents talking about the Shantymen's Association was around the time of my grandfather's funeral. Percy Wills was the Shantymen's Christian Association minister who used to stop and visit Ivan and his family at Hot Springs Cove in the *Messenger III*. He was just a few years older than Ivan and grew up on Caledonia Street, where Royal Athletic Park in Victoria is today, very close to where Ivan grew up. Chances are pretty good that Ivan and his siblings would have known him from school. Percy raised his family right around the corner from where my father grew up in Victoria.

Ivan's first wife, Beatrice, never remarried, despite several men showing romantic interest. She passed away at 100 years of age in 2003. She is interred in historic Ross Bay Cemetery in Victoria. Their eldest child, Beverley, and her husband, Barry, are interred with Beatrice. Raymond was interred with his grandmother, Annie Emma (Carlow) Clarke, also in Ross Bay Cemetery.

Ivan, his second wife, Mabel, and four of their children, Billy, Art, Jimmy and Buddy, are all buried in the Seaview Cemetery in Tofino. Diane is buried in Regina. Hugh's wife, Maggie, is buried in the Ahousat Cemetery.

Major George Nicholson wrote, "Ivan's venturesome establishment of the settlement of Hot Springs Cove and Maquinna Provincial Park can now be found on any map of Canada, and the world. Not very many people have been able to lay claim to such an accomplishment. Ivan was able to look back on his life with satisfaction, at a life that few of us will ever achieve." The Ivan

H. Clarke and Sons company was dissolved in September 1973, about two years after Ivan passed away, but was re-established for a while a year or so later to finish settling Ivan's estate.

When I was very young, I knew all about my grandfather's second family but did not have the opportunity to meet them until I was in my early twenties. At that age it was very interesting for me to meet people who resembled my mother. After years of procrastinating, I first visited Ahousat in late August 2015 and had a great visit with my uncle Hugh, my cousin Iris, her husband Tom and their daughter Shelby. I visited again a month and a half later, getting in more visiting time with Uncle Hugh, and asking him even more questions. Planning ahead to get the most time possible at the hot springs, I took a water taxi from my uncle's float at his general store out to Hot Springs Cove in the early morning and back again in the late afternoon. It turned out to be an unbelievably hot, sunny October day.

While visiting Ahousat, I had a chance to chat with several of the locals and was very humbled to hear the kind words they had to say about Hugh, which echoed the words said at Uncle Art's memorial at Port Alberni early in 2013, about Art, Hugh, Ivan and the extended Clarke family in general. People came from near and far to attend. They spoke words that sent a tingle

Hugh Clarke, shown in front of his Ahousat general store in 2015, shared many stories about growing up at Hot Springs Cove. Iris (Clarke) Huebner Collection

up my spine. Ivan's was a kind, generous family and highly respected by all those in the surrounding communities and all those who knew and visited them from near and far.

In the very early 1970s, when I was in my teens, I can remember cutting my grandfather's lawn at his house on Balfour Avenue in Victoria, which was very close to where I live today. In his garage, beside the door to the backyard, was his old table-top metal lathe. He offered it to me, but I said I was a woodworker and would not know what to do with a metal lathe. I kick myself to this day for not accepting his offer. I was, however, given his 1960s Buren wrist watch, as well as his mother's 1893 Waltham pennant watch, which I passed along to my daughter, Olivia, engraved with all the previous owners' names, upon her 2017 university graduation.

Right about now I think Ivan has a twinkle in his eyes and a big smile on his face and is probably having a really good chin wag with his grandson, Captain Richard Clarke Oldow, who attended the US Merchant Marine Academy in Kings Point, New York, for two years, but did not like the East Coast, so he transferred to the California Maritime Academy in Vallejo, California and graduated from there. Richard worked in the towboat industry, operating tugs in Alaska, the Pacific Northwest, Gulf of Mexico and the Great Lakes. He joined Ivan in the heavens in 2007, after passing away in Springfield, Missouri.

Museum Donation

While conducting research for his thesis on prehistoric use of thermal springs in the Pacific Northwest, Dennis G. Griffin drew upon an archaeological survey of the area around Hot Springs Cove conducted in 1973 by David Coombes. According to Griffin, Coombes stated that the site occupied by the Clarkes, identified as Borden number DiSn2, "contained a shell midden with whalebone, and a stone hammer was known to have been collected from the site that was in the possession of the Clarke family at the time of recordation." Coombes's informant regarding the site was Art Clarke.

At least one other artifact had been found at the site. In 1948, Ivan donated a bone war club to the Royal BC Museum. Grant Keddie, Curator of Archaeology, described the approximate 17.25-inch (43.7-cm) whale bone club as "missing the proximal or handle end." He went on to say that the club "shows two figures that I interpret as lightning snakes. Lightning snakes were the thunderbolts of the thunderbird, used to kill whales." The most likely date range for the club is between 300 and 900 years old.

David Coombes first visited Hot Springs Cove in 1968, Ivan's last year there. When Coombes spoke with Art Clarke during his 1973 survey, it was the last year a Clarke family member was working and living at Hot Springs Cove.

Park Expands Slowly:
Hot Springs an Issue

Several decades passed between the initial establishment of Maquinna Provincial Park with the land Ivan and Mabel had donated and the park's expansion, which included the hot springs. Several more decades later, it expanded even more into Maquinna Provincial Marine Park.

Almost 13 years after Maquinna Provincial Park was officially established in January 1955, Tofino-area MLA Dr. Howard McDiarmid was talking about expanding it into a marine park. In early December 1967, McDiarmid announced that he was happy that Ivan had donated land for a park, but it did not stop his plans for a marine park, although he did note that the Clarke donation had not included the hot springs themselves.

Admitting that in winter the area is "rough, rough, rough," and that such a park would be open to boating in good weather months only, McDiarmid went on to say that he would push for a west coast national marine park when the next session of Legislature opened.

The Wyllie Land

Ever since Ivan and Mabel's parkland donation, the provincial government had been urged to buy southern Lots 486 and 697, consisting of about 1.5

miles (2.4 km) of coastline owned by Robert Wyllie. He owned half of the
water rights to the hot springs, but Wyllie was an absentee landowner (in the
1970s he was living in Florida). The government was holding the other half of
the water rights in reserve.

In 1967, the two lots were priced at $75,000. Over the following years
they went up to a high of $350,000 then back down to $200,000, as well as
various other prices in-between. The two lots were situated at the southern tip of Openit Peninsula. Due to the location of Wyllie's property below
Ivan's property, the Ahousaht Reserve No. 27 and Maquinna Provincial
Park, Wyllie's property was now landlocked. Other than using the trail
through the park, the Wyllies had no real way to get access to their own
property. In the meantime, when people went out to use the hot springs,
they had basically been trespassing for all the years that the Wyllies owned
the property.

In late 1973, when the Wyllies put their two lots for sale through a Vancouver real estate company, represented on the island through Tartan Realty
of Campbell River, there was a flurry of letter-writing internally between
ministries, different government agencies, political clubs, organizations,
real estate agents and private citizens on why buying the hot springs would
be a "fantastic acquisition for the government." Although the government
agreed with the sentiments, they had already spent their allocated funds for
that year. One of the sales pitches came from Bob Skelly, MLA for Alberni,
in an October 1973 letter to Robert H. Ahrens, director of the Parks Branch
for the Ministry of Recreation and Conservation. Skelly promoted Ran-
dall Fielder, a citizen from Tofino who managed a successful charter boat
business carrying passengers between Sydney Inlet and Clayoquot Sound.
According to Fielder, the route between Tofino and Hot Springs Cove was
popular amongst tourists. Skelly suggested that the success of Fielder's venture was "indicative of the public's interest in the hot springs as a recreational area."

Just a year before this, the Long Beach to Port Alberni logging road was
finally fully paved, creating Canada's only paved road to the open Pacific
Ocean. Tofino thus became the official terminus for Island Highway 4, and
the unofficial Pacific terminus for the Trans-Canada Highway.

In his 1973 letter, Skelly mentioned that the government's reasons in
the past for not purchasing the hot springs had been the remoteness of the

land and the high cost. Now, he reasoned, with the government becoming increasingly active in acquiring parklands, the money could be made available. Knowing that in the past the Parks branch had been extremely reluctant to use the minister's power to acquire land, he felt it was time for the government to take steps to purchase this land "before it was lost to public use."

At this same time, Minister of Agriculture Dave Stupich sent a memo to Minister of Recreation and Conservation Jack Radford, enclosing some information about the hot springs location supplied by one of his constituents, wanting to know if Radford knew anything about them. He wondered if it was something that the government should acquire before it was purchased by another Canadian or non-resident.

In a letter dated December 18, 1973, from a Mr. Lionel J. Kirkham living on North Pender Island and sent to Robert H. Ahrens, the director of the Provincial Parks Branch, it was noted "that it would seem to be to the public's advantage if the present government hurriedly purchased the hot springs property and incorporated it into Maquinna Park." There was no need to develop the property right away but, as Kirkham reasoned, the hot springs could become a popular tourist feature much like Radium Hot Springs, another hot spring on Vancouver Island. He also mentioned that there was no road access, and a road would not be needed right away if they created a "slashed and blazed trail" through the 20 or 30 miles (32 to 48 km) from Gold River. He figured that the walk would be good exercise for people and put them "in tired shape" to make the hot springs all the more enjoyable.

There was also internal government correspondence mentioning that additional money from the Green Belt fund could aid in purchasing the two lots to add to Maquinna Park. In a December 27, 1973, internal memorandum sent to Radford was a report on why purchasing the hot springs was a bad idea. It said that the terrain would be difficult to develop, the shoreline was too rocky and exposed and the hot springs too small. The report further went on to highlight other issues.

> If the site is acquired for a park, we can foresee management problems. Objections will surely arise from the present practice of mixed nude bathing and the only method to control this would be to staff this isolated hotspring [sic].

The report suggested that the asking price of $150,000 would be better used acquiring other potential park lands such as Spider and Horne lakes, which were also in the Alberni District.

There was also discussion early in 1974, wondering if the development of the hot springs and a bathing facility, both costly endeavours, was an appropriate task for a public agency to take on. If a private developer were able to develop the hot springs and then charge a small fee for the use of the hot springs, the cost of developing the springs would be borne by the people who would actually use it, rather than those who wouldn't have the opportunity to. The government, it was decided, should apply public funds in such a way as to "provide maximum benefit for the public." Charging people to use the hot springs was the exact opposite of what Ivan and Mabel intended when they donated the land to forever give the people of British Columbia free land access to the hot springs.

In a January 12, 1974, letter to Ken Farquharson, the founder of the Sierra Club of British Columbia, Recreation and Conservation Minister Radford stated that the Parks Branch thoughts on purchasing the hot springs property remained primarily unchanged. "The Parks Branch has many other properties throughout British Columbia with higher recreation potential that must be purchased first."

The Parks Branch land acquisition funds were extremely limited and so it was difficult for them to justify spending so much money on acquiring park land that would benefit so few people. Although Radford agreed that the property had intrinsic value as a natural phenomenon on the west coast, he stated that other areas of the province needed recreational land even more than Vancouver Island at the time. He concluded that the purchase of the hot springs would be considered "a misuse of their available funds."

This reasoning was reiterated by Robert Ahrens in a letter to Mr. S. Anderson, secretary for the Coombs–Parksville NDP club, dated January 31, 1974.

Although this property may be desirable, it is not high on our list of purchase priorities as the recreation potential is limited due to the small size of the spring. The pools only hold approximately ten "friendly" persons and because of the limited flow and location are unsuitable for development.

Its purchase at this time would therefore be difficult to justify, especially at the present asking price of $150,000. As there are many other properties throughout B.C. which would have greater potential, it is our considered opinion that the money would be better spent elsewhere.

Ahrens's letter was in response to the latest meeting of the NDP club, which had passed a motion to send a letter "to ask the Director of the Parks Branch, to purchase the land at Hot Springs Cove that encompasses the hot springs, so that the springs will belong to the people of British Columbia." They asked for an early acknowledgement of their request and an approximate date of when they would make the purchase.

Government Gets Serious

Robert Waugh Wyllie passed away at 74 years of age on March 1, 1974, in Broward County, Florida, where he had resided for many years.

Although the government had pondered cancelling Wyllie's water licence for non-use, it did not seriously try to acquire Lot 486 consisting of 45 acres (18 hectares) and Lot 697 consisting of 20 acres (8 hectares), which contained the hot springs and pools, until after 1974.

On July 28, 1975, Parks Minister Jack Radford sent a letter to Agriculture Minister David Stupich, advising him that the purchase of the Hot Springs Cove property was being negotiated through the Department of Lands and Forests and that they were dealing with Colette Zuber Wyllie, who was the administratrix of the Wyllie estate.

Finally on August 12, 1975, the provincial government purchased Clayoquot Land District Lots 697 and 486 from the Wyllie estate for $85,000. That November 30, the *Daily Colonist* included an article about the purchase of the park written by Major George Nicholson. As part of his article he wrote:

Notwithstanding the fact that it will be years before the park is developed and its inaccessibility by car, surprising is the number of people, especially during the tourist season, who insist on going there anyway, by boat from Tofino.

Over 15 years later, on December 21, 1990, Maquinna Park was expanded to include the entire southern end of Openit Peninsula by Order-In-Council 1933. Through Bill 53, the Park Amendment Act of 1995, the area was expanded to Hesquiat Harbour and the name of the park was changed to Maquinna Marine Park.

Maquinna Marine Park Today: *Springs a Big Attraction*

M aquinna Marine Provincial Park is now approximately 6,590 acres (2,667 hectares) in size, including 3,136 acres (1,270 hectares) of upland and 3,454 acres (1,398 hectares) of foreshore. Tens of thousands of visitors get to experience the park and the hot springs each year. In 1953, before Ivan and Mabel even donated the land, more than 500 people were counted heading out to the hot springs over one summer weekend, mainly off of the fishboats. In 1990, approximately 2,500 parties visited the hot springs, and in the summer of 2016 there were approximately 350 people a day visiting from all over the world. The hot springs are now a major tourist attraction, one of the most popular day trips out of Tofino by boat or float plane, and rated among the top ten natural hot springs in Canada. Maquinna has been classified as a Class A park. Such parks, in the words of the BC government, are "lands that are dedicated to the preservation of their natural environments for the inspiration, use and enjoyment of the public." Development in such parks "is limited to that which is necessary for the maintenance of its recreational values."

Maquinna is also designated as a Provincial Marine Park, defined by the BC government as a park "administered by the province mainly for water-oriented activities and may or may not be only accessible by boat."

Maquinna Marine Provincial Park is one of the most popular day trips out of Tofino.
Diane Kaehn photo

According to a February 2003 provincial government document on the Maquinna Provincial Park Purpose Statement and Zoning Plan, the primary role of the park is "to protect and showcase special values such as geothermal and geological features. The park protects a significant hot spring on Vancouver Island and its associated hot temperature ecosystem, a unique underwater vent, and sea caves. The upland hot springs provides a focus for recreation and tourism to both visitors to and residents of Clayoquot Sound."

As of April 1, 2017, the Ahousaht First Nation signed a 10-year agreement with the provincial government to manage Maquinna Provincial Marine Park. This agreement means that the Ahousaht First Nation is in charge of the daily operations of the park. Their purpose is to greet guests and maintain the facilities of the park, as well as help create more of an Indigenous presence in the area. After arriving at the Hot Springs Cove government wharf, it is a relatively easy 1.25-mile (2-km), 30- to 40-minute walk to the geothermal hot springs (depending on your age and physical condition) along a cedar boardwalk with 793 stairs (one way), which leads through a luscious and thriving old-growth forest. Often, visitors will glimpse moss draping over the lower branches of the trees and carpeting the forest floor, creating a magical sight. In the summer of 2015, my then 83-year-old Auntie Pam (Ivan's former daughter-in-law) and her daughter, Linda-Rae, walked the length of the boardwalk out to the hot springs, but Pam decided it best not to chance clambering over the rocky outcrops to access the pools themselves.

Originally, the trail came out onto the hot springs much lower than it does now. The only real cutting down of big trees was around the Hot Springs Cove settlement itself, which is noticeable in pictures of Ivan's operation taken from the water in early days during the 1930s and '40s. The rest of the pristine rainforest was left intact, other than improvements to the trail to the hot springs. The trail is now bordered by various rose and wild berry bushes, as well as ferns and wildflowers of all kinds. The hot springs are situated 150 feet (45.5 m) from the west shore of Sharp Point, about 1,000 feet (303 m) from the outer end and about 50 feet (15.2 m) above high-tide level. At the springs,

Visible in the centre of the photo, hot water bubbles to the surface of the pool at a temperature of 125F (52C). The water slowly cools as it makes its way through the six natural pools before flowing into the ocean. Diane Kaehn photo

gas bubbles continually surface right at the fissure and the springs give off small quantities of methane, nitrogen and hydrogen sulphide. Depending upon which way the wind is blowing, one can catch the rotten-egg smell of the hydrogen sulphide from a fair distance away. The smell is an indicator that the water is slightly acidic as it comes to the surface, but the sulphur content in the water is actually quite low.

The spring and the six natural pools that the water flows into after tumbling down a waterfall are basically untouched and are still, today, in their natural state, although visitors over the years have tried using rocks to make the pools larger and deeper, as well as having left evidence of using candles to add a bit of romantic atmosphere while they were soaking in the pools in the evenings.

The rate of flow of 100 gallons (454 L) per minute and temperature of 125F (52C), have remained constant since they were first officially measured in 1898. Close to 6,000 gallons (27,240 L) of hot water cascade down through the natural pools to the ocean every hour of the day and night. The steam can sometimes be seen rising by passing boaters, especially on cooler days.

Close to 6,000 gallons (22,700 L) of water cascade through the pools each hour. The rate of flow has remained constant since it was first officially measured in 1898. Diane Kaehn photo

These days, you can see the viewing platform/change house on the east bank as you come up the cove, which quickly gives away the location of the hot springs.

A Provincial Park sign located near the viewing platform out at the hot springs reads:

Created over 160 million years ago under extreme fire and pressure the "igneous" and "metamorphic" rocks of Hot Springs Cove (Refuge Cove) reveal this as a place of dynamic geological activity. This part of Vancouver Island rests on an unstable portion of the earth's crust, known as a "fault." This major fault, extending offshore from Mate Island, north along the west side of Hot Springs Cove to Hesquiat Lake, is associated with intense heat and pressure generated from deep within the earth. Maquinna Park's main feature, Sharp Point Hot Springs, ranks as a major thermal spring in Canada, with a high water discharge of about 5 to 8 litres per second. The hot springs are a result of surface water flowing through a "fault" to a depth of 5 kilometres. The water is geothermally heated to a temperature of at least 109 degrees C before hydrostatic pressure forces the water back to the surface and discharges through fractured rock at a temperature of 50 degrees C.

Sitting in the hot springs, as far as one can see to the east and west there is rugged, densely wooded coastline, in a not-soon-to-be-forgotten panoramic view. Depending on the weather, there could be huge white-capped waves breaking up on the rocks below with a mountainous roar and showers of blowing spray. Flying in the winds are different species of snipe and oyster-catchers that forage the shoreline, or herons, osprey and eagles waiting for a feeding of fish. In the kelp beds, which mark out submerged rocks, the head of a seal might suddenly appear, or there might be a huge sea lion or two or three sunning on the rocks.

It is a good place to see stern trawlers, seiners, trollers, gillnetters, packers and longliners disappearing in and out of view in the ground swells, or large ships passing by. In this day and age, one can also see numerous water taxis, chartered and private boats, as well as float planes coming and going, picking up and dropping off residents and visitors to the cove.

Hugh recommended people to start at the bottom-most pool before slowly moving to the upper pools. When the tide is high, the cold ocean sloshes into the lower two pools, where a person can sit and experience both the cold salt water from the ocean and the hot sulphur water from the spring, which is both unique and invigorating. It is quite the sensation to sit in the bottom pool when the tide is coming in and the waves start pushing the cold water into it.

The cold water entering the bottom pool starts coming in slowly with the rising tide, but thanks to the ocean rollers straight from Japan, during the highest part of the tide, you can be sitting waist deep in the bottom pool enjoying the hot sulphur water flowing past, and in seconds the cold ocean salt water surges in up to your neck. It's pretty cold, but thanks to the hot water already in the pool, it is bearable. As quickly as the water rushes in, the pool empties. This tidal action of alternating hot and cold water in the lower pools usually lasts for about an hour and flushes out the lower pools twice a day during high tide. This process lasts longer after storms, which make the tides higher. As far as is known this phenomenon does not exist in any other hot spring in this part of the world.

On calmer days when the tide is out, Nicholson wrote, "One can explore the shore for mussels, sea urchins and seashells of every size and shape including fan-shaped scallops and wonderfully coloured abalone, which can

The rocky shoreline at the hot springs remains largely unchanged since Ivan's day. Diane Kaehn photo

be found in the crevices. Sea stars can be seen and hours can be spent exploring the tidal pools." He went on to say that there were few populated places in BC where the spectacle of the sun disappearing over the horizon could be viewed so clearly, and that sunsets at Hot Springs Cove were quite the spectacular sight. If staying that late, one needs to be sure to take along a good flashlight, as it is a long hike out in the dark.

Ghost Town

Even though Ivan once had a number of buildings and installations ashore at Hot Springs Cove, in 2019 the site where his business was at the cove could almost be called a ghost town, except that it was never really a town or village of any significant size. It was, though, a very important stop on the west coast of Vancouver Island in many people's lives, and a thriving fishing community unto itself. Almost nothing remains of the dozen or so buildings today that would indicate just how big Ivan's operation—or "Old Man Clarke's"— was at the end. If Ivan's ghost was going to hang out anywhere, it would be right there by the slate cairn with the "Maquinna Provincial Park" dedication plaque, to cheerfully greet visitors when they get off the Hot Springs Cove float/wharf, any time of the day or the night, in any kind of weather, at any time of the year, as they head off on the boardwalk to the hot springs.

Little of Ivan's once-expansive operation remains at Hot Springs Cove, now the entrance to Maquinna Marine Provincial Park. Diane Kaehn photo

The park has grown and changed since Ivan's donation in 1959, but it remains a treasured place of recreation and enjoyment for British Columbians—and visitors from all over the world. Diane Kaehn photo

As much as I tried, no one was able to provide me with any numbers regarding the financial impact that the donation of land by Ivan and Mabel to the people of British Columbia has had on Tofino and surrounding areas, but one can only imagine it is in the millions of dollars every year.

ACKNOWLEDGEMENTS

Fortunately for me, my mother kept every newspaper article and all the old pictures of my grandfather, Ivan Clarke. My mother's siblings and cousins were ever so generous, passing along information and sharing photos, as well as answering my many questions about life at the cove.

At about 14 pages, my friend Susan Allen edited and proofread the manuscript, as I thought I had everything in order for a submission to Harbour Publishing for their Raincoast Chronicles series. But unexpectedly, my story kept growing.

Scott Thornton of KLA Registry Services Ltd. helped me locate my grandfather's and Wyllie's land grants. Thanks to my long-time friend Earl Warnock, who has a wealth of knowledge of BC land grants and preemptions. The wonderful staff at the British Columbia Archives helped me, as did the fine people at the Maritime Museum of BC and the Vancouver Maritime Museum.

Tofino historian Ken Gibson was very helpful, freely telling me about his memories of my grandfather, as well as sending me historical pictures of Ivan and Refuge/Hot Springs Cove from his vast collection. Thanks to the highly recommended "The British Colonist" online search site where I was able to find many historical newspaper articles that mentioned the cove and my grandfather. Dave Christensen of Tofino helped me sort out when Art Clarke and his parents worked together. The late George Nicholson wrote many newspaper articles about my grandfather. His grandson, Colin, and I had a chat and he divulged great information, which I have added. John MacFarlane, and his "Nauticapedia" web page, was an extremely helpful resource. Dave Minshall helped me solve the question of how tugs operated their auxiliary systems after converting to diesel power. Many thanks also go to David Lynch, whose last-minute information helped clarify some details in the book.

When I emailed my manuscript to my cousin and author, Bob Collins, in Port Alberni, he thought that it was a story that a very well-known West Coast publishing company might be interested in, tactfully not once mentioning whether he thought I had writing skills or not.

My friend Alison Makkinga, who had previously edited and proofread books for a small, local publishing company, offered to proofread and edit my finished manuscript.

Many thanks to all my contacts at Harbour Publishing: substantive editor Cheryl Cohen, who turned my manuscript into a readable book; copy editor Patricia Wolfe, who fine-tuned the book; Rebecca Pruitt MacKenney, who went over all the historical photos with me; and Marisa Alps, Harbour's marketing manager.

During this more than five-year journey, I have certainly crossed paths with a long list of individuals, whose assistance added that much more to my book. I could not have finished it without them. I am ever so thankful to all those I have mentioned or alluded to, whether I have named them or not.

Michael Kaehn
Victoria, British Columbia
December 2018

SELECTED REFERENCES

Books

Dorricott, Linda, and Deidre Cullon. *The Private Journal of Captain G. H. Richards*. Vancouver, BC: Ronsdale Press, 2012.

Findlay, Alexander George, F.R.G.S. *A Directory for the Navigation of the North Pacific Ocean*. London, England, 1870.

Lillard, Charles. *Mission to Nootka*. Sidney, BC: Gray's Publishing, 1977.

Nicholson, George. *Vancouver Island's West Coast 1762–1962*. Victoria, BC: Morriss Printing, 1962.

Online References

Barr, Debra. *Tofino Livesaver*. B.C. Historical News, Volume 13, Number 3. 1980. https://open.library.ubc.ca/collections/bch/items/1.0190738#p3z-5rof:barr

Griffin, Dennis G. *Prehistoric Utilization of Thermal Springs in the Pacific Northwest*. 1985. https://ir.library.oregonstate.edu/xmlui/bitstream/handle/1957/9414/Griffin_Dennis_G_1985.pdf?sequence=1

Langer, Shirley. *Tofino Profiles: Art Clarke*. Tofino, BC: February 2005. http://www.tofinotime.com/articles/A-T502-30frm.htm

Legion Magazine. *The Japanese Threat: Impounded On The West Coast*. 2011. https://legionmagazine.com/en/2011/09/the-japanese-threat-impounded-on-the-west-coast-navy-part-47/

MacFarlane, John M. *The Nauticapedia Project Vessel Database*. 2014. www.nauticapedia.ca/dbase/Query/dbsubmit_Vessel.php

MacFarlane, John M. and Lynn Wright Salmon. *Flotsam, Jetsam & Lagan: Stuff for the Receiver of Wreck.* Nauticapedia.ca, 2002. www.nauticapedia. ca/Articles/Articles_Receiver.php

Maritime Museum of BC. *Graveyard of the Pacific: Tales of Hope and Courage.* 2004. www.virtualmuseum.ca/edu/ViewLoitCollection. do?method=preview&lang=EN&ID=21168

Mertl, Steve. BC *Government Expresses Regret Over 1869 Aboriginal Hanging Deaths.* 2012. https://ca.news.yahoo.com/blogs/dailybrew/b-c-government-expresses-regret-over-1869-aboriginal-215249641.html

Rough Radio, British Columbia's Coast Station History. Stranded Barge. www.roughradio.ca/albums/bowerman/426_450_wjb.html

The Hot Springs Cove Story contains information that has been derived from the information originally made available by the Province of British Columbia at http://www.bclaws.ca/ and this information is being used in accordance with the Queen's Printer License-British Columbia available at http://www.bclaws.ca/standards/2014/QP-License_1.0.html. They have not, however, been produced in affiliation with, or with the endorsement of, the Province of British Columbia and THESE MATERIALS ARE NOT AN OFFICIAL VERSION.

Additional Sources

Daily British Colonist, Victoria, BC, various, 1874–76

Daily Colonist, Victoria, BC, various, 1877–1975

Ha-Shilth-Sa, Port Alberni, BC, various, 2010–15

Ladysmith-Chemainus Chronicle, Ladysmith, BC, February 1, 1978

Maritime Museum of BC, Victoria, BC

Province, The, Vancouver, BC, April 5, 1958

Royal BC Museum and Archives, Victoria, BC

Spokane Chronicle, Spokane, Washington, May 30, 1988

Times-Colonist, Victoria, BC, August 31, 1997

Twin City Times, Port Alberni, BC, March 17, 1965

Vancouver Maritime Museum, Vancouver, BC

Victoria Times Colonist, Victoria, BC, various, 1900–1971

Victorian, The, Victoria, BC, September 19, 1975

INDEX

Page numbers in **bold** refer to illustrations.